1. Monogram used for personal stationery (see fig. 119)

Permission to reproduce previously
published designs by Neville Brody is
gratefully acknowledged (for details
see p. 160)

Set in Franklin Gothic Demy and Book roman
and italic (text 8/10 pt, captions 7/8 pt)

First published in the United States of
America in 1988 by RIZZOLI INTERNATIONAL
PUBLICATIONS, INC. 597 Fifth Avenue,
New York, NY 10017

ISBN 0-8478-0934-X
Library of Congress Catalog Card Number
87-63121

Printed and bound in Spain by
Artes Graficas Toledo S.A.
D.L. TO—1827—1988

THE GRAPHIC LANGUAGE OF NEVILLE BRODY

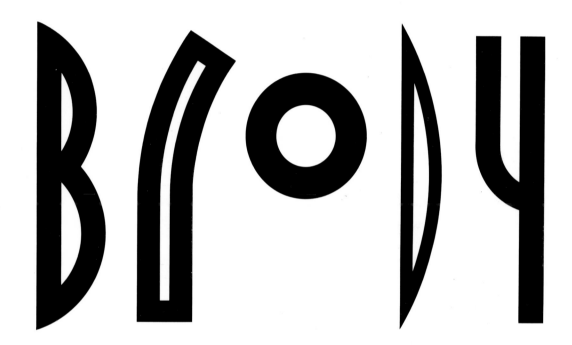

TEXT AND CAPTIONS BY **JON WOZENCROFT**

With 474 illustrations, 101 in full colour

RIZZOLI
NEW YORK

CONTENTS

INTRODUCTION

In 1988, Neville Brody is the best-known British graphic designer of his generation. His record cover designs have been highly regarded but most of all his work on magazines, notably *The Face*, has transformed the way in which designers and readers approach the medium. Magazines have become of even greater importance to advertising and commerce in the last seven years as carriers of consumer information. Inevitably, their stylistic developments have had a direct effect on High Street shop design, on art and television – upon every area of the visual communications industry.

The Graphic Language of Neville Brody therefore goes further than to merely assemble the published work of its designer subject. Since the early days of *The Face*'s success, Brody's graphic work has been widely imitated with scant regard for his original intentions. This book sets out to restate these intentions, whilst staying conscious of both the advantages and the pitfalls of hindsight:

Such clarification is necessary; whether fact, belief, gossip or opinion, all information in the media has become interchangeable and based on disposability. When style rather than content is the driving force of a culture, as it is today, it requires a keen eye to differentiate the original from its countless simulations.

'Signification' has become a habit – in design, it is an easy way of appearing to share a common language without avail to any meaning except its commercial familiarity. Since Brody has never sought to make his work obscure, it becomes even easier to replicate; its ideas have then been codified and represented through those codes alone. *The Graphic Language of Neville Brody* tries to reveal their hidden trace.

Neville Brody grew up in Southgate, a suburb of North London. The place is in-between two environments – the nearby neon lights of London's West End, and the Hertfordshire countryside which starts at the end of the Piccadilly tube line; Southgate, whose station won architectural awards for its 1930s circular design, is two stops down the line. Suburbia creates such contrasts, and in spite of its orderly roads and cul-de-sacs, at its heart is also the promise of transformation.

At school, Neville Brody studied A-Level Art, very much from a Fine Art viewpoint. 'I don't remember a time in my life when I was going to be doing something else. Ever since I had any self-awareness, I've wanted to do art or painting'. Consequently, in 1975 Brody went on to do a Fine Art foundation course at Hornsey College of Art, once renowned for its late Sixties agitation, now safely amalgamated into Middlesex Polytechnic.

Brody's experience of the Fine Art mentality at Hornsey was a mixed blessing. In marked contrast to the Situationist stirrings of 1968,[1] the college was by now well reconditioned to the provision of 'good students' – i.e., those who would have no trouble getting work. What he witnessed here was the way the establishment had learnt to deal with rebellion. There was no student movement to speak of, and Brody was being exposed to nothing that one would readily associate with the rebellious upsurge made public in 1976. 'The reverse was true – I was feeling that within mass

communication, the human had been lost completely. I wanted to understand the everyday images that were around me at that time, and the process of manipulation particularly within commercial art. By understanding the mechanism at ground level, I hoped to produce the opposite effect by turning them on their head.

'The big decision I took at this stage was whether to follow Fine Art, or to pursue Graphics. I felt that the Fine Art world had become élitist and would appeal only to a specific gallery market; my time at Hornsey did nothing to dispel this feeling, so I thought Graphics would offer better possibilities. I thought "why can't you take a painterly approach within the printed medium?". I wanted to make people more aware rather than less aware, and with the design that I had started to do, I was following the idea of design to reveal, not to conceal.'

In autumn 1976, Brody started a three-year B.A. course in graphics at the London College of Printing, its main building an ominous tower-block in London's Elephant and Castle, a nightmare of inner-city planning. Here it was rumoured that the college turned out people who could hand-draw a page of text so that it looked as if it had been printed by a machine – unlike the lurid graffiti that coloured your walk every morning through the underpass from the tube station to the college.

'I wanted to communicate to as many people as possible, but also to make a popular form of art that was more personal and less manipulative. I had to find out more about how the process worked. The only way possible was to go to college and learn it.'

Although the LCP did have a strong crafts background, Brody felt its atmosphere to be repressive and stultifying. His tutors condemned his work as 'uncommercial', once again preferring 'safe' economic strategies to experimentation.

'I was at the LCP during a period of transition, away from the basic belief in the Bauhaus[2] attitude that you pursued Fine Arts like drawing and printmaking, first, to find out about the techniques involved, and secondly, to bring a different understanding of communication to your design work. They had some great facilities at the college – the old Daily Mirror printing press (1906 vintage, I think), screen printing, Monotype[3] and computer typesetting machines, and a colour xerox machine that cost only 20p a copy. Then, all of a sudden, we were being taught that the only reason for doing a life-drawing or any experiment in printing was to come up with a motif that could be translated and extended into an advertising project or record cover design. The college was no longer interested in ideas for their own sake.'

By 1977, Punk Rock was beginning to have a major effect upon London life[4] and, as far as Brody was concerned, this provided the catalyst he needed. 'My designs went in for servicing and came out supercharged. I'd gone to the LCP because it had a reputation for being the hardest graphic design college in Europe, not hard as in difficult, but pure. I felt that if you wanted to react against anything, you had to learn about that thing totally, but the LCP was giving me nothing but grief. Punk hit me fast, and it gave me the confidence I needed. What really did it for me was Wire's *Pink Flag*,[5] and especially what they said at that time – that you should pursue an idea, do it, stop, then go on to the next one.'

2. *Sputnik*, college fanzine, 1978
Brody's early experimentation with type and image (see fig. 7).

Brody's designs did not go down well; at one stage he was nearly thrown out for putting the Queen's head sideways on a postage stamp design. He did, however, get the chance to design posters for student concerts at the LCP, most notably for Pere Ubu, supported by The Human League, when the latter was one of the principal exponents of the cinematic live performance, an area they shared with fellow-Sheffield group, Cabaret Voltaire, with whom Brody would later work. In 1977, 1978 and 1979, many groups were experimenting with film and video alongside their music, experimentation whose original ideas were far removed from what pop video has become, even if many of its idioms have since been absorbed by the new form.

Brody was not alone in his frustration with the distance between college work and what was happening at large: 'Ian Wright, who was in the year above me, was also at odds with his tutors; his work was fantastic and very influential upon mine. He had a very illustrative approach to type, yet he was totally misunderstood and accused of a lack of commercialism to a far greater extent than I was. I was still concentrating on imagery, and putting all my energy into using type in a similar way. We had another thing in common — both of us worked really hard, because at least then you couldn't be dismissed for lack of application.'

In spite of the deviant postage stamp design, Brody was not only motivated by the energies of Punk. His first-year thesis had been based around a comparison between Dadaism and Pop Art: 'Dadaism embraced the means of the destruction of art, and set against the carnage that was taking place in World War I, it was saying that art too, in its previous role, was dead. It was a period of crisis when art was looking to itself and saying "why does art exist?", "why paint?", but of course there is no why. (*Why not sneeze, Rrose Sélavy?*) In a certain sense, art died with Dadaism — with Duchamp and his 'ready-mades'. It reached the ultimate statement that art is whatever you say it is, and if it still refused to lie down and die, then it had to look around and embrace other areas.'

'We "painted" with scissors, adhesives, plaster, sacking, paper and other new tools and materials; we made collages and montages . . . It was an adventure even to find a stone, a clock-movement, a tram ticket, a pretty leg, an insect, the corner of one's room; all these things could inspire pure and direct feeling. When art is brought into line with everyday life and individual experience, it is exposed to the same risks, the same unforeseeable laws of chance, the same interplay of living forces. Art is no longer a "serious and weighty" emotional stimulus, nor a sentimental tragedy, but the fruit of experience and joy in life.' (Hugo Ball, *The Language of Paradise*, 1917)[6]

Dada was 'anti-art' where art manifested itself as an industry without any relevance to the common man; of itself, it was probably the most artistic of any intervention this century. Futurism, its historical companion, was also influential upon Brody's work, more for its typographic experimentation than for its philosophies and attitudes. 'The work of Boccioni also inspired me. The Futurists embraced the new technology of their day, but it was more as a means of survival — in any case, they soon showed where their true sympathies lay. Marinetti, in particular, was keen to glorify Mussolini's *fascisti*. Pop Art, on the other hand, whilst it was very influential on Punk, was really a commercial art and this it promoted in a way that made anti-commercial images acceptable.

'Pop Art was a vindication and a celebration of the commercialism that developed out of the Fifties. You would see Andy Warhol's electric-chair sequences in the same context as the flowers, the soup-cans, and the Marilyn Monroes: his art was subversive for about fifteen minutes. In effect, he aided the homogenisation, and at the end of the day this is what made him so successful. Rauschenberg, whose work was more challenging, never reached that public.' Writing about Lichtenstein's comic-strip paintings, Hans Richter commented in his essay 'Neo-Dada': 'The feelings they evoke in the beholder's mind belong to the artistic level of the garden dwarf.'

In Brody's view, 'If you look at Man Ray's and Duchamp's work, they had already fully explored the basis of Pop Art in two or three works — likewise, Hans Arp, Magritte and Richter himself. Pop Art was a marketing exercise that had more to do with the imposition of modern cultural United States than with experimentation. It was a mass-producible culture that could dominate the international scene out of the sheer volume of its coverage, its simulations and its instantaneous referral to pleasure.

'With the advent of photography in the nineteenth century, the social role of painting was replaced. Art was made redundant, but not in the way that the Dadaists would later have liked it. Since the 1920s and 1930s, art has lost its direction, and most people are simply restating ideas already covered fifty years ago. This pleasure-seeking is, on the one hand, a flight from the more obscure aspects of 1950s Abstract Expressionism, but it's got as much to do with simple laziness. The nadir really came in the 1970s Structural Minimalism. That's what I would say is "anti-art". It's anti-human.'

Stepping forward to 1988, architecture has entered the dialogue once more as an artform as well as a mark of social policy. Prince Charles' often timely comments notwithstanding, architecture has been the traditional scapegoat of the new, yet at the same time (with reference to this medium's own recent history of failed Modernism) it is desperate to get back into the picture. The term 'architecture' in the context of graphic design was explored by E. M. Farrelly in an article written for *Architectural Review* in 1985, very much with the above reservations in mind. Entitled 'The New Spirit', Farrelly's article marked a path from the graphic work of Neville Brody in the last ten years back to Dadaism and Constructivism, making connections through the magazine as a whole with the work of Barney Bubbles, Malcolm Garrett and Jamie Reid, amongst others. The article also spoke of 'the death of Post-Modernism' — its observations about this genre's artificiality were timely and accurate.[7]

Much of today's architecture depends on blending the correct historical reference to the right modern noise (from digital sampling in sound to the conglomerate aspirations of inner-city development). During the late 1970s, Punk highlighted industrial and social decay not only through its iconography — groups being photographed outside building sites and shopping centres, for example — but with the use of xeroxes, echoed human degradation through the degradation of process: the xerox was a mechanised form of communication whose end result looked as rough and as quickly thrown together as Punk's product. Fanzines[8] were another part of the shift that was going on, in the way that they opened up a distribution network that did not (at the time) have to rely on multinational systems. Where this connects to architecture is not within a traditional category; it refers to a state of mind that does not always see one medium disconnected from the other, whilst at the same time celebrating the differences between, say, photography and painting, sound and colour — categorisation, after all, exists mainly for the benefit of salesmen and social observers. As a way of illustrating one's concern for the whole of the environment, architecture is meant more as metaphor. Categorisation, like censorship, now comes increasingly *before* the act of transmission.

Once consolidated, style culture in Britain was ideally suited to the prevailing Tory ideology. Ideas, with Punk, that had found their expression outside were replaced by those that worked on the inside. This was no self-questioning attitude, but a style that had to be seen inside clubs, in the right shops, and in the right clothes. A culture only recently based on the quest for ideas and a sense of being turned to the surface values of the body and the look. For those who were excluded (both by virtue of limited purchasing power and, more importantly, because of their access to the media's output but never its source), this ritual was about the domestication of man and time.

3/4/5. College Briefs, 1978/79
Record cover; magazine cover; inside page.

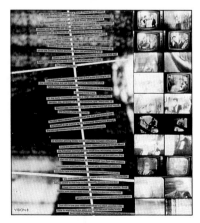

'If ritual is best seen as an organised way to harness power or to make things happen, performed along rigid lines but evading conventional "rational" analysis, then its most powerful expression now rests in a place and form that is still barely recognised. Today's rituals are not carried out personally or from within a small community, but through a mass central repetition and reception. They are not performed by shamans or purifying spirits, but by venal agents — the Right Wing cartel that runs the newspapers and is now setting its sights on broadcasting. The effect of these rituals is not to bring about a specific personal or group awareness, but to bring a seeping loss of power to the mass.' (Jon Savage, *Touch Ritual*, Touch, 1986).

' "The Media" has become the religious faith of the late twentieth century, and its editors, stylists, designers and programmers have become the high priests. Today's environment is saturated with media scenery and thoughts, the High Street a battleground, requiring always a passive, non-reactive response — other than to purchase. Britain's main success in export has been the selling of its style. In the mass-production of the commercial marketplace, the further manipulation of media that are by their very nature already manipulative has resulted in a blandness and a violence that can only increase the misery of modern man.'

When we are all conditioned to compare ourselves with a media-projected image of 'man' or 'woman', and when the people who are creating such images base their latest projection on the lowest common denominator of the previous one, one's initial instinct might be to meet one kind of terrorism with another. Brody has always chosen to work, however realistically, from the strongest possible position of influence *within* the media. His response to the media's power was to develop a personal idea of tribalism where the intention is to reintroduce the human form, and human markings, into the visual environment. This tribalism might be thought of as 'modern primitivism' — not such a contradiction as it may seem; it expresses the most pressing task of the day, for mankind to rediscover the idea of a personal destiny rather than to be forever controlled by external influences. Most graphic designers of the 1980s allow themselves to be marketled, an irresponsible attitude that does nothing to offset the drabness of the High Street, and the feelings of inadequacy that it promotes. Brody felt that the only way to effect public understanding was to influence the people in power, namely other designers. Brody, however, not only overestimated people's desire to look beyond the surface of things, he had not yet come to terms with the greed of the design industry, who saw the success of his experimentation as ripe for plunder, and not as a cause for self-questioning. A sense of responsibility becomes even more imperative to written content, images and the space they occupy. Design as architecture *has to* become design as ecology.

The catalyst of Punk had not been able to sustain itself, principally because its architects could never keep pace with the latest High Street re-fits. London's Virgin Megastore, for example, has changed its in-store design countless times since it opened in the late 1970s. By that time, the groups at the heart of Punk's intervention were filling the racks there in a different costume. As catalysts, this is where Dadaism and Punk part company. Whatever assimilation Dadaism has undergone in the last seventy years happened to Punk in the space of about seven months. Dadaism's greatest triumph was that it was an attitude that could always be shared, but an outcome that could never be copied. In the case of Punk, it was something nearer to the opposite; an

6. College brief for fishing float package, 1979
Brody was learning to react intuitively to a brief: rather than taking the expected illustrative approach, he chose to apply an expressive graphic sensibility to a commercial subject.

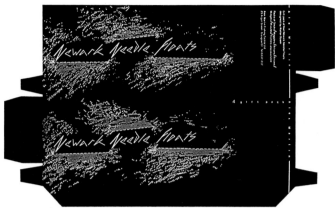

intervention that easily passed into style, where the new protagonists need share nothing of its original intentions.

'The New Spirit', then, is a starting point, and should be valued for its emphasis on a shared objective and the beginning of something that is not immediately captioned as a collective 'movement'. What the article omitted to make clear was that the principal connection between architecture and design is as simple as the latter's emphasis on a three-dimensionality to counteract surface values. There is, as I have suggested, another side to this question that relates particularly to the experience of *The Face* magazine. Brody's response to this began with his college work, however, and what he calls 'Pattern as Hypnosis'.

This relates to the area of three-dimensionality in Brody's work via two distinct areas of influence, one literary, the other artistic. Firstly, his response to the media's hypnosis is to introduce the 'random factor', an idea that comes more from the work of Brion Gysin and William Burroughs than from Dadaism. The Dadaists, even with the knowledge of their many effective provocations, were at the time always more interested in 'winding people up' than they were in becoming the legendary figures that they now are.

Brion Gysin's invention of the 'cut-up' grew into a collaboration with William Burroughs that they called *The Third Mind*, a means of connecting two apparently unrelated elements to create a third 'meaning' that is based on the intuitive over the reasoned — although paradoxically, the third 'result' might contain infinitely more reason than the sum of its two parts. The background to this work is well documented elsewhere[9] — basically, 'The Third Mind' can be seen as a way of confronting the *language problem* peculiar to today's media world of soft focus and hard sell. In Brody's work, 'The Third Mind' is applied to design by contrasting elements, with the use of the accidental as a way of counteracting the conformity of modern communication systems. However, the accidental is never in itself sacrosanct.[10]

The second area that had a large influence on Brody's work can be seen in the photograms of Man Ray and Laszlo Moholy-Nagy, and in particular, through the diverse artworks of Alexander Rodchenko. The Constructivism of El Lissitsky and Kasimir Malevich made an impression that at one time was equally vital,

7. Typeface One, 1979
Brody's first typeface design already showed an illustrative approach to letterforms. The type, based on a system of bars of three different weights and limited angles, highlighted the most readable elements of the characters.

8. Poster for Pere Ubu/Human League concert at the LCP, 1978
The poster, screen-printed by Brody, used a found image and typographical style that broke with LCP tradition. Reminiscent of an age when consumerism and its styles promised a glorious future, the montage was typical of its time – Fast Product, the Human League's first record label, would often use such images on record covers.

9. The Motors, 'Love and Loneliness', Virgin Records, 1979
After joining Rocking Russian, Brody's first single sleeve design highlighted a graphic approach to the emotive subject matter.

though their 'Supremacy of pure sensitivity' is ultimately more enclosed within the newly established Soviet Russia of the 1920s than it is relevant to 1980s England, in spite of 'CCCP' T-shirts where revolution becomes style. Man Ray's poetic photographic forms and 'wrapped objects' such as *L'Enigme d'Isidore Ducasse* hold, in their surrealist language, many of the keys to modern-day advertising's manipulative techniques – though with none of the beauty of the original. Laszlo Moholy-Nagy, a participant in the Bauhaus of the 1920s in Germany, believed in the 'unconscious education of man', not from a pedagogic standpoint, but from an awareness that even if his chosen medium of the photogram might to some be simply 'pleasing', then its deeper impression would, in time, be recognised. Moholy-Nagy, like Man Ray, de-fined many of the limits of photographic form that have yet to be surpassed. Both described themselves as painters rather than photographers, and both, in spite of their differing images, rec-ognised the value of photography as the manipulation of light before its form became concentrated on the manipulation of its documentary status, which, in reality, more often appeals to an impulse that replaces memory.[11]

Alexander Rodchenko subverted the notion of the artist as specialist by experimenting with a wide variety of artistic areas to question the boundaries between them; he applied himself directly to the language of everyday life in the Russia of the Twenties in his work on posters, photographs and book jackets.

In 1988, 'design' has for many people become a dirty word, symbolising the superficiality of cosmetic solutions which show contempt for deeply-entrenched problems. For Rodchenko, de-sign was a means of the artist coming between his work and the needs of his public: a design to interact. As Khan-Magomedov writes: 'The contradiction between experimentalism and the need to communicate with the public at large during the early Soviet years was readily perceived by Rodchenko, but he also came up with a possible solution to it. In fact, Rodchenko's "Abstract" language can legitimately be interpreted as the expression of an unusual determination to establish a dialogue with the public, to make each operation undertaken on language itself potentially explicit, by renouncing the mediated representation of reality and by transforming the materials, immediately, into form, into a medium of communication.'[12] With reference to Gysin and Bur-roughs, collaboration takes on another dimension.

One point that needs to be stressed is how quickly the herit-age of avant-garde design can be disengaged and its meanings converted into style. We cannot have a full idea of what exactly these meanings were, not having lived in Moscow in 1924 or Zurich in 1917; the battle, however, is now more extreme, be-tween ideas and experimentation and their supposed denial of the professional result – what is wanted by Business. Again, it is the shift from divergence to conformity.

'The difference, I think, between the way I approached Dada-ism and Constructivism is that I never sought to copy their work, which a lot of people were doing at the time. I looked at it and tried to evaluate the core of what was being done, and why. What I took from it was a sense of dynamism, a sense of humanism and a non-acceptance of traditional rules and values. Once you looked at that, you could then pursue your own response. I have always felt that the last fifty years of design have been recycling these already explored areas.

'I was influenced by Herbert Spencer's *Pioneers of Modern Typography*, and the work done by the magazine *Campo Graphico* in Italy during the 1930s – especially the design of Max Huber. The experimentation that *Campo Graphico* undertook in the print medium becomes even more impressive when you consider its context.' Attilio Rossi, the magazine's editor from 1933 to 1935, later wrote: 'It was to our advantage that we represented a precise and conscious ethic of opposition to Fascism. We were opposed to the idea of modern printing, a highly effective means of com-munication, being used to spread lies.'[13]

Brody also thought that Jan Tschichold (author of *The New Typography* in 1928, much imitated as a Modernist aesthetic) was an establishment figure. 'He was effectively trying to find new rules to apply to this experimentation. His work normalised typography in much the same way as David Bowie normalised 'new wave' to a great number of people, and although within the music business Bowie never had to live with the rules, with typography today we are still living with Tschichold's rules — look at Penguin Books.

'As for design in 1979, I was most impressed with the work that Barney Bubbles was doing for the small independent company, Stiff Records, where I would work soon after leaving college; and Al McDowell, who had a design company called Rocking Russian, operating mainly in the music business. By the time I was set to leave college, I saw this area as the only one that would offer any chance of experimentation, and I thought the point of doing a final-year thesis was, in the main, to help me to get a job at the end of the course.

'I had been aware of monthly magazines by the French group, Bazooka (La Graphique Résistance),[14] and especially *Bulletin Périodique* that subversively illustrated a news story taken from each day of the preceding month. With the fanzine boom going on, there were many others but the one that really held my attention was *Grabuge*, produced by Al McDowell; my thesis was on magazines, so I went to interview him — at this stage, however, I had no intention of working on magazines.

'In any case, Rocking Russian had been started essentially to do the sleeves for the Rich Kids, ex-Sex Pistol Glen Matlock's band. Al McDowell had previously been responsible for the printing of the 'Destroy' T-shirts for Malcolm McLaren, and he had completed a Fine Art course at the Central School of Art and Design: I thought his approach to work was very similar to mine. I did my thesis, and the day after the show was taken down, I went to work for Rocking Russian. I was there for nine months, a time of absolute poverty while living in a squat in Covent Garden. Rocking Russian was very expressive on a creative level, but business-wise, it was possibly the worst-run institution I've ever been involved with.

'Record covers really were the boom industry in design at that time. There was a supportive network to enable an interesting sleeve to reach anything from 10,000 to 50,000 people. I thought the record shop was just as valid a showcase as the framed environment of art galleries, or, better still, that your living room was a place to look at and think about visual expression, without any of the dogma of a gallery. I thought that Stiff Records was adventurous in its design and marketing; I liked Barney Bubbles' and Chris Morton's work, so after leaving Rocking Russian, I went to work at Stiff for a year.

'What I had not realised was just how clever a piece of marketing their whole operation was. Really, Stiff was the first independent label that tried to emulate the major record companies, and while I was developing the idea of "putting man back into the picture", I was getting very frustrated by the manipulation that I was witnessing at first hand. What kept my sanity intact was the fact that I had met the group 23 Skidoo and, as a consequence, Rod Pearce, who was then setting up Fetish Records. This eventually gave me the chance to get out of the mainstream and work on the things I really wanted to. Anyway, I soon had to change course — Stiff sacked me, but we won't go into that here!'

Working between two elements, allowing each their individual expression, is difficult to maintain. From a designer's angle, the viewer is left with the choice intact, in contrast to the usual design practice of presenting a *fait accompli. The Graphic Language of Neville Brody* sets up some of the problems to be questioned; Brody's design itself has never sought to present solutions to the viewer. The need, therefore is to continually expose assumptions — and to incorporate a process of self-challenge. Brody's over-riding intention has always been to encourage the viewer to look twice, but in many cases, the reader-public has not had the inclination to take this any further. If a degree of subsequent confusion is the price one has to pay for this 'independence', it can also be thought of as Brody's response to the ever-increasing method

of *the merger* — a phenomenon that applies not only to multi-national companies, but to the divergence of life itself. Communication is today more complex than even an understanding of 'the process' can fully uncover. So we are led to believe.

'Increasingly, meanings and attitudes are transmitted and made memorable by aural association — the jingles, the oohs and ahs of modern advertisement — and by the pictorial means of billboard and television. The read sentence is in retreat before the photograph, the television shot, the picture alphabets of comic books and training manuals. More and more, the average man reads captions into various genres of graphic material. The word is mere servant to the sensory shock. This, as McLuhan has pointed out, will modify essential habits of human perception. Three dimensional colour television, able to communicate happenings from one part of the earth to any other with instantaneous drama, will not only erode further what is left of private silence, but educate the imagination to an avid passiveness.'
(George Steiner, 'Literature and Post-History', 1965, in *Language and Silence*, Faber and Faber, 1967)

1 'In 1957 a few European avant-garde groups came together to form the Situationist International. Over the next decade the SI developed an increasingly incisive and coherent critique of modern society and of its bureaucratic pseudo-opposition, and its new methods of agitation were influential in leading up to the May 1968 revolt in France'. (From *Situationist International Anthology*, edited by Ken Knabb, The Bureau of Public Secrets, 1981). The SI's best-known tacticians were Chtcheglov, Débord and Vaneigem — they believed that the best way to provoke change was through the 'construction of situations' that would lead to the end of the 'alienation of the old world, built on the ruins of the modern spectacle'. Their main enemy was boredom.

2 The Bauhaus was an arts, crafts and design school set up in Germany in 1919 by the architect Walter Gropius. Lasting until Hitler's appointment as Chancellor in 1933, its lifespan was precisely that of the Weimar Republic. Frank Whitford, *Bauhaus* (Thames and Hudson, 1984), gives a summary of this period. See also Kandinsky, *Complete Writings on Art* (Faber and Faber, 1982) and Paul Klee, *The Thinking Eye* (Lund Humphries, 1961).

3 The Monotype Company was the largest supplier of type founts during the letterpress era, before lithography became the dominant printing method in the 1950s. Their machines — also manufactured by Linotype — were elaborate typewriters used by compositors to 'cast off' type into galleys which were then arranged into the 'forme' that would make the printing plate for 'hot metal' letterpress machines. Letterpress uses a 'relief' printing plate, whilst lithographic plates are photographically etched.

4 An important feature that distinguished Punk from the style movements that were to follow in the 1980s was its provincial nature. In 1977, events in Manchester, Liverpool, Edinburgh, Bristol etc. were just as crucial as those in London. In 1981, only London had enough nightclubs to sustain the party — that is, if the doorman would let you in.

5 Wire, *Pink Flag*, EMI Records SHSP 4076. The LP was released in Dec. 1977 on EMI's subsidiary label, Harvest — also the outlet for Pink Floyd and many other 'progressive' groups of the late Sixties and the Seventies.

6 Quoted in Hans Richter, *Dada — Art and Anti-Art* (Thames and Hudson, 1965). This book is still the best available introduction to Dadaism.

7 Arguments continue to rage as to what, exactly, is meant by 'Post-Modernism'. Its exponents chose to combine any elements they felt like including — a category to end all categories. Unfortunately, this also ushered in a great deal of self-indulgence and a new age of Pluralism. Jon Savage (*The Face*, No. 80) asked 'How can you kill off something you never understood in the first place?'.

8 'Fanzine' is short for 'fan magazine'. *Sniffing Glue*, edited by Mark P, is the best-known of the Punk era.

9 Aside from *The Third Mind* itself, see also Gysin/Wilson, *Here To Go: Planet R-101* (Re-Search Publications, 1982; reissued in 1986 by Quartet Books).

10 It is doubtful whether Gysin and Burroughs intended their cut-up technique to be used as a gimmick — which is what it in fact became with the introduction of studio 'sampling' technology in the early Eighties (cf. the group Art of Noise and Paul Hardcastle's 1984 number one, *19*). Also when cut-up is over-used as an effect, for example in the genre known as 'Scratch Video', its choice of material which usually comes from TV news becomes as manipulative as the source it seeks to question. What it does is to promote pastiche, not parody.

11 See Susan Sontag, *On Photography* (Allen Lane, 1978), and John Berger, *Ways of Seeing* (BBC Penguin Books, 1978).

12 S.O. Khan-Magomedov, *Rodchenko* (Thames and Hudson, 1986).

13 Rossi had refused to publish posters for the Fascist plebiscite in Italy. He later wrote: 'One of the posters said literally: "In 1950, Europe will be decrepit: the only young country will be Italy — Mussolini!". Nowadays, no one needs to be told that it was a lie.' (Rossi, in *Campo Graphico*, Electra Editrice, Milan, 1983).

14 La Graphique Résistance was a non-political group of French illustrators, including Lulu Picasso, Kiki Picasso and Olivier Clavel, amongst others. Their work was largely financed by left-wing political groups, though *Bulletin Périodique* never allowed this to inhibit its critique: indeed, one of the group was shot in the knee-cap for daring to bite the hand that feeds. In France, Punk did not take the form of music — it was visually expressed.

10. Desmond Dekker, *Black and Dekker*, Stiff Records, 1980
An illustration based on a photograph, one of Brody's first covers for Stiff. The typography shows an early Constructivist symmetry in Brody's design.

TYPOGRAPHY

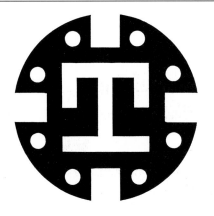

had set my own brief at college. I complied with the curriculum requirements because I needed the chance to explore those ideas too. I was acutely aware that this was the only time I was likely to get to follow ideas before having to go out and look for work, where I'd have to think on my feet. Employers certainly wouldn't let you spend three months studying a photographic process, and if we did, we'd starve. The whole art college system collapses when all members of staff are full-time, and when they fail to recognise that it is not they who have to go out and find a job afterwards. They fail to recognise the need to help develop a student's individual talent. Instead, everybody is moulded into an expected way of being; colleges aren't geared towards producing pioneers but gauge their success on professional imitation. If tutors said they liked something that I was doing, I would go away and change it, because such approval then made me think there must be something wrong with the work. I think that was a very positive and healthy attitude to take.

'I hated my time at the LCP, but I value it. I cannot emphasise how important it is for people to be encouraged to explore ideas, and then to be encouraged to work on them. One of the results of recent staff cut-backs is that students are left to swan around, they're not pushed, and it's not right.

'What college teaches you is design as problem-solving, in the sense of design needing to please rather than to invent. You are taught to solve a problem, which is to take the short-cut of satisfying expectations, and this is not the same as meeting your public halfway. Design is no different from art, or chairs for that matter. As a means of communication, it cannot remain neutral.

'At the root of it, design is a language just as French and German are languages. Whilst some people are able to understand design fluently, there are those who just use phrase-books. They don't understand the words they're using, but the phrase meets their need. Up to a point, you have to use a common language, and to meet people at least halfway. That's why going to college was so crucial for me, to understand the process of seduction and turn it against itself. For a lot of designers *The Face* became the perfect graphic phrase-book, but its success, I hope, is also an indication to students at college now that you can go against the grain and make it work commercially.

'Communication exists on far more levels than the simple communication of an idea, but I can't see it as problem-solving. You become a scientist, a technician, performing a service. What that does is to destroy the emotion of communication, which is the thing that is most lacking in the first place. Painting is not seen as problem-solving. If you approach design from the point of view of problem-solving, then essentially it is the problem that you are communicating.'

'Design is emotive, yet it's taught as if it were non-emotive. So at college, I started from the basis of how you intuitively react to a project. The problem is not to signify emotion but to be emotion. If your reaction to a brief is rational, then trust to that, and if it's an emotional response, trust to that. If you take design as problem-solving, then you might say "this product needs to emphasise speed", so what you do is find a way of signifying speed — you don't trust an emotional reaction to it, and the signification is

11/12. Symbol and poster for *Touch*, 1987
Printed dark blue on recycled sugar paper, the poster was intended to announce forthcoming releases by *Touch* — the type needed to be striking (having decided not to use half-tone images, which in any event do not reproduce well on such a stock), communicating a continual movement and rhythm. The hand-drawn type is contrasted with industrialised symbols, and the flow of label information is based on the reversed letter 'S'. The 'dial' symbol ensures that distribution details are easy to find.

THE LEGE·NDARY

14. Poster for the group Out, 1983
A contrast between the broken-down quality
of the type and the sharpness of the smaller
symbol. The design indirectly suggests '007'.

**13. Symbol for a video
production company, 1983**

inevitably going to be weaker than the actual. Design is taught as representation, and that's really the extent of it. With what's going on in society today, this representation just compounds the misery.'

ALMOST ORGANIC. Our journal of this day presents to the public the practical result of the greatest improvement connected with printing since the discovery of the art itself. The reader of this paragraph now holds in his hand one of the many thousands of impressions of The Times newspaper which were taken off last night by a mechanical apparatus. A system of machinery almost organic has been devised and arranged, which, while it relieves the human frame of its most laborious efforts in printing, far exceeds all human powers in rapidity and dispatch. That the magnitude of the invention may be justly appreciated by its effects, we shall inform the public that after the letters are placed by the compositors, and enclosed in what is called the forme, little more remains for man to do than to attend upon and watch this unconscious agent in its operations. The machine is then merely supplied with paper: itself places the forme, inks it, adjusts the paper to the forme newly inked, stamps the sheet, and gives it forth to the hands of the attendant, at the same time withdrawing the forme for a fresh coat of ink, which itself again distributes, to meet the ensuing sheet now advancing for impression; and the whole of these complicated acts is performed with such a velocity and simultaneousness of movement, that no less than 1100 sheets are impressed in one hour.
(From *The Times*, 29 November 1814, reprinted in Humphrey Jennings, *Pandaemonium – The Coming Of The Machine As Seen By Contemporary Observers*, André Deutsch, 1985)

The following is taken from a discussion between Neville Brody and Jon Wozencroft, July 1987.

'In the West, the Roman and Greek alphabets provide the basis of the consciously designed letterform, but you can carry this further back to the Ancient Egyptians' use of hieroglyphs or even to ritualistic markings in caves. At what point does true typography begin?

'The Modern Tradition in typography really begins in the fifteenth century with the birth of printing. The basic rules of set type haven't changed since then. The rules, however, should not be seen as a limitation — everything should be challenged through a natural process of questioning — and if there is a practical reason for any design element to exist, and it is still relevant to what you intend and there is no alternative to it, then that element remains valid. What you are left with is there for reasons of tradition, rules that exist purely on the grounds of taste, or ideas that, since they've been around so long, have become accepted as rules. But there is no grounding for such things other than what we are used to. Take the writing of William Burroughs — he uses words that convey meanings, but the normal traditions of sentence structure completely break down.'

'In that case, what factors govern the design of a magazine?'

'The page grid is the basic skeleton, from which you hang everything. It's equivalent to the scaffolding, or the walls and the joists of a building. A grid is crucial — there has to be enough space incorporated in such a way that you don't get the impression that things are being thrown out from the centre of the page. It has to create an enclosure without interrupting the flow from spread to spread.

With *The Face*, on the most simplistic level, we decided that a

magazine needs to show the reader where a specific feature starts, that it has a certain number of consecutive pages, and that it is followed by another feature. You decide to have a contents page to act as a key — it's an advert for the magazine, a second cover, equivalent to the back of a book jacket where you read the blurb. The contents page tells you what and where each feature is; the practical element is that you use numbers on each page. Tradition seeps in when you come to consider what typeface should be chosen for those numbers, what size they will be and what position on the page they will occupy. That is totally open to question; you might even use symbols instead of numbers.

Take another point — you want to encourage people to read an article. You have to indicate where each article starts. But the way you start an article can take any form you like, as long as you're still indicating the beginning by directing the reader's eye to it. You can use a symbol, a form, or a different typeface; you might even use white space; you can use any means. Certainly with *The Face*, that was one of my greatest obsessions — the signposting facility of typography. An easier way to understand this process is through something like town-planning.'

'When you are signposting the beginning of an article in a very expressive way, do you not think you are in danger of over-involving the reader with the signposting at the expense of what is being signposted?'

'The signposting should work on a subliminal level — it's not supposed to function as the most obvious element. The basic structure of *The Face* was one of manoeuvring the eye and the intellect — the signposting was doing the passive work for the reader, but what those signs looked like was creating a reaction; I was laying open questions, pointing out the manipulative nature of how signposting works. Traditionally, you don't. The use of an initial dropped capital is the accepted way of doing it, but an abstract shape can have the same function. Taking that idea a step further, we would enlarge the first few words of an actual text and use them in headline form to lead the reader's eye straight into a piece. Once you have broken down the rules, literally anything is possible.

Quite clearly, I was not offering any solutions in *The Face*. I was pointing out questions. I was pointing out approaches and attitudes, realisations that you could break things down to their raw elements, and then rebuild them with an awareness of their function. I never tried to hide the signposting — the reverse was true.

Consider headlines. A headline grabs the reader's attention on a certain page and articulates the message "This is the beginning of a new piece, it's about something that is different to the piece before, we want you to read this, so we have to give this page in the magazine a certain amount of weight." That is your basis, but there are other ways of doing it — you could use white space with a very small headline, smaller even than the main text. By doing that, having questioned the headline rule, once again anything becomes possible. Unfortunately, with the use of a small headline, people took that as the establishing of a new rule.'

'In recent times, people have desperately clung to tradition, and style affords it to those who are not prepared to invest time in finding out for themselves what is worth regenerating and what must be transformed.'

'I think it's a fear of mortality, quite honestly. The way style

16. Demop logo, 1985
The design was never used – Demop, a London hair salon, thought it 'too religious'.

15. Kopf logo, 1985
Hand-drawn logo for a hat company.

EXPO

EXCERPTS FROM *BRUCE WEBER*'S PHOTO-JOURNAL

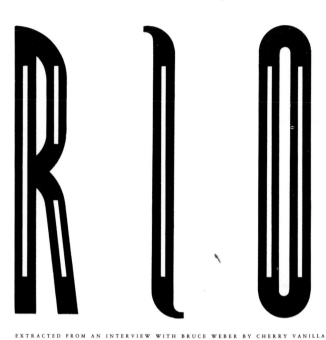

O RIO

BRUCE WEBER'S *O RIO DE JANEIRO* PUBLISHED BY ALFRED A. KNOPF, AVAILABLE SEPTEMBER. ALL PROCEEDS TO THE AIDS RESOURCE CENTRE. PHOTOS FROM THE BOOK ON SHOW AT THE ROBERT MILLER GALLERY, NYC, FROM SEPTEMBER 9

SURF GANG, PRAINHA

PHOTOGRAPHS BRUCE WEBER

STYLING JOE McKENNA

HAIR DIDIER MALIGE

MAKEUP LUIS MICELOTTI

EXTRACTED FROM AN INTERVIEW WITH BRUCE WEBER BY CHERRY VANILLA

"I said to Bob Miller, 'Bob, isn't it weird that I'm doing this photographic journal, about young kids in Rio and romance, and sex, and going to the bar and getting drunk, and whatever, and I'm donating the money to the Aids Resource Centre?' I mean, that may sound a little bit whacko, but uh . . . There's a crazy thing going around now, people are really frightened, they're frightened of expressing themselves physically because of all the disease that's happening. And I think they're getting really paranoid and overtly prejudiced for *any* kind of sexual reaction. Everybody should be paranoid a little bit, and be on their guard, but I think that to deny the romance in your life is just the worst. And why I feel more and more strongly about the Rio book is that the people in Rio have this thing when they first meet you, they kiss you. Men come up and they hug you, and girls come up and they kiss you on the cheek. They're not making a pass at you. It's their way to say, 'Hi, I'm here. It's okay if you touch me. You can talk to me.' And they have a wonderful acceptance about people's fragile sexual sense. They're very much like children in that way. You go to a bar with your friends, and on one side of you there'll be a drag queen, and on the other side, there'll be a Rambo. And it's all the same to them, you know. They have that kind of adaptability. They find romance in everything. And I just find it so frightening, that all these people here (New York) are just losing all the romance. This book is mostly about romance, I guess. It's about the spirit of Rio really, and the young boys and the young girls of Rio."

THE FACE

17. Feature for *The Face*, No. 77, September 1986
A visual article by Bruce Weber on Rio de Janeiro with one piece of continuous text. The hand-drawn 'Expo' logo was intended to strengthen the piece by contrasting its digital look with cosmopolitan subject matter, challenging the traditional idea of how a feature should look.

DEMOB ATTIRE

DEMOB ATTIRE

FISHMONGERS
47 BEAK STREET
LONDON W1

01 437 9007

THE GREAT GEAR MARKET
85 KINGS ROAD
CHELSEA
LONDON SW3

NEW YORK OFFICE
(212) 460 5278

DESIGNERS

(LONDON)

ROBIN ARCHER
P. WINTERS
SARAH LUBEL
DIANE GARROD
SUZANKA FRAEY
SUE GLASS

(NEW YORK)

JON BAKER

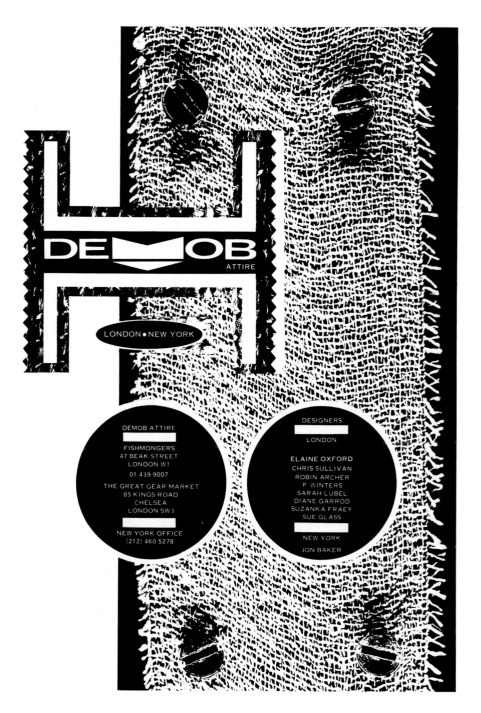

has manifested itself in British contemporary culture is really as a fear of age, a fear of looking old. "Youth Culture" was the key catchphrase of the early Eighties for a great area of the media.

With typography, the fact that we are now saying "these are the problems, these are the rules, here are other ways of doing it", means in a way that we are falling into the same trap that *The Face* fell into — by pointing out examples of possible alternatives, those examples are taken to be rules.'

'*What was the catalyst that turned you from working predominantly on images with record covers for Stiff and Fetish to working through typography on* The Face?'

'There's a crucial reason — until I started working on *The Face*, there was enough freedom and flexibility within the record industry for me to be able to express the same ideas, but within imagery. I was able to use this imagery to communicate my thoughts, and how I wanted people to react to them. After the all too brief interruption by Punk in the late 1970s, the industry geared itself much more towards commercialism for commercialism's sake. The validity of using a surprising image on a record cover disappeared. What was wanted was a photograph of the band together with straightforward type. If you did use a different sort of image on a record cover, it was assumed to be part of an existing language, and it was no longer a surprise or a thought-provoking exercise.

This development coincided with my first work for *The Face*; I had never in my wildest dreams intended working on magazines, never. I'd always dealt with images — with type, but as an integral part of the image-making process. Suddenly, with *The Face*, I was confronted with typographic problems. In my very early work for

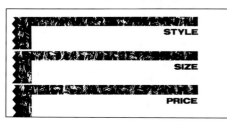

18/19/20/21/22. Range of advertising, price-tag and clothes label for Demob, 1982/83
Brody used and extended the tactile quality of the clothing, stripping it to a graphic form without illustrating the product itself. The strong shapes and cloth-cut edges expressed a distinctive feel for the shop.

The 'M' of Demob was based on the idea of a military motif, which offset the perfume-like oval of the 'London-New York' line.

23. Demob carrier bag, 1984
Demobilisation was the name of Demob's second shop. The design implies World War II industrial engineering: the main shape might be taken as a submarine or a petrol station sign.

24. Trouser patch for Demob, 1984
The heroic symbol was based on a Welsh miner in preference to the ubiquitous Wild-West cowboy.

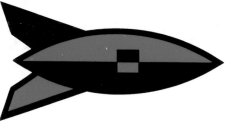

25/26. Launch poster and invitation for Harvey Nichols, 1985
The rocket symbol is closer to Dan Dare than High Street fashion shops. The design suggests mock-camouflage.

27. Revue, clothes shop, proposed logo, 1983

28. One Off furniture, 1983

29. Fred Bare, hat company, 1985

30. Comag, magazine distributors, proposed logo, 1986

31. Square Yard, warehouse club, 1985

32. Fwa Richards, choreographer, 1987

33. IPART, Institute of Photographic Apparatus, Repairers and Technicians, 1983
An updating of a previous design.

the magazine, I was still trying to orientate the design towards the use of imagery, bringing in hand-drawn drawings (not a tautology these days), like the tape recorder box on the "Funkapolitan" spread (see fig.76).

I suddenly found myself out of necessity having to try to get the same emotive impetus from the way I used type. I hated type. It was out of frustration, because I was falling into the trap of treating type in the same way as everyone else. I thought typography was a boring field to work in, overladen with traditions that would repel change.'

'Were you aware of these traditions at this point?'

'No, I was fearful. At college, I had rejected Typographic Studies, virtually out of hand. I just found the subject incredibly boring, and I assumed it to be a practice of intellectual perfection, not one of emotive communication. I was scared of using type then, because I felt (and I still do in many ways) totally incompetent at typography. Because I missed that traditional training, I feel that somehow I'm not a real typographer. But that has also been an advantage — I haven't been tied down at all. When I started working at *The Face*, I had no respect for the traditions of typography, because I had no understanding of them. But I did understand what I saw around me — I did have an admiration for the typography of the Dadaists, Futurism, and Rodchenko.'

'Is there anything about the typographic traditions you have since learnt that has been of value?'

'The traditions of typography are not fun; communication should be entertaining.'

'But if you design to be entertaining, too often you only succeed on the basis of entertainment — of which there's more than enough already.'

'No, not if it's purely entertaining. If you look at typography now, modern, trendy High Street fashion shop typography, that's what you're referring to as hollow — it's using words in the same way as you would use a strange shape. It has connotations, but it isn't actually saying anything — and wide-spaced, condensed, sans-serif typography doesn't say anything, it merely signifies. Where I think it's valid with *The Face* is that primarily the magazine is about entertainment, but there was a very serious reasoning behind it. It wasn't used as surface style — the style evolved from a breakdown of the traditional structure.

If you break down a traditional structure, it can go in one of several ways: it can be flat and boring; it can alienate through its jarring with what is normally accepted; or it can actually entice attention through its entertainment value. The majority of people were not aware of what *The Face* was doing and dismissed the ideas and the seriousness behind it.'

'Do you think it was the entertaining aspect of your typography that encouraged so many people to try to emulate it?'

'I wanted people to emulate the breaks with tradition that I was making. I didn't just want people to copy the examples I'd chosen to use. The actual choice of typeface in any particular context is secondary to the way in which the typeface is used.'

'Taken from another viewpoint — with hand-drawn type, where the master is done on graph board, there are only so many variations that you can get from that grid system before the result becomes badly composed hand-drawn type.'

'But your creativity should counteract this. I've always tried to work to the best of my abilities, and within my limitations — I wouldn't know how to draw Baskerville, for example. What I was trying to point out was that people shouldn't feel limited to the range of typefaces made available to them by typesetters. Hand-drawn type was a reaction against the growing use of computerised setting, where you didn't need to know anything about type to create something interesting from it. With CAD (Computer-Aided Design), reliance on the tool is a growing phenomenon. I suspect the real craft — aside, this is, from the tradition — is now a dying ability; in addition, with the advent of desk-top publishing, a typographer can now be the laziest person in the world. It's so easy, you don't even have to specify things to size, because you

34. Zuice logo, 1987
A band logo that has been adapted on various
record releases (see figs. 177, 178, 179).

can get it "set to fit", or PMT[1] to enlarge or reduce accordingly. The whole Letraset boom in the Sixties was symptomatic, not casual, of this trend. Computer typography, as it is presently used, is no more than the next step after Letraset. Instant Design Letraset grew out of the American advertising boom of the Fifties, and is now the normal way of things. You don't even question it — you just say "Where's the Letraset?".

In fact, we started using Letraset on *The Face* because I wanted more immediate control of what each individual letter looked like. I was using Letraset for all the headlines. Then I found I could manipulate the Letraset. I could easily combine letterforms from different type families and alphabets. As I grew in confidence, I found that I could change things and it became a creative process rather than a mechanical one. I introduced other elements like hand-drawn signs and symbols into the lettering, sometimes replacing the letters altogether. I could cut off bits of a letter, or squash things together. I had total control, and it was more like working with paints than with something normally seen as a mechanical form.

The belief in the truth of computer-aided typesetting is really a blind alley. The greater the belief in the truth of a tool, the less freedom you have in using it, because once you become a slave to technology, you're lost. A slave in the sense of the belief in the truth of technology. Technology, ultimately has to be a tool. It is not an end in itself; it is not the content.'

'The eye is always a much better judge of letter-spacing than a set computer instruction.'

'That's right — but I must admit that if I look at a headline that I spaced last year, I usually feel that I now want to space it differently!'

'What made you choose to letter-space type even at very small point sizes?'

---

1 PMT = Photomechanical Transfer, the means by which drawings/designs/images are photographed onto bromide paper to create camera-ready artwork for the printer. Photocopies can, of course, be used, but the result will not be as sharp-edged.

PAUL KLEE

35/36. *Opposite:* **Promotional material for 'Jazz at the Manor' festival, 1985**
The design was based on a modular system that allowed for adaptation into any format — a system that other designers have since found useful. Brody chose not to use traditional Jazz imagery, but instead developed a more dynamic typographic representation.

37/38. Promotional material for Paul Klee exhibition at the Museum of Modern Art, Oxford, 1983
This design broke with the previous style of the Museum's newsletters by using large wide-spaced vertically-placed type together with a clear visual structure. The newsletter folded to provide a front and back cover.

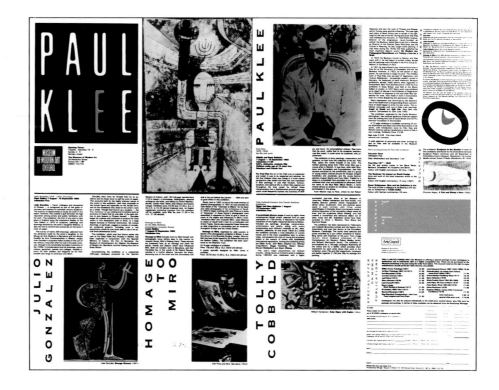

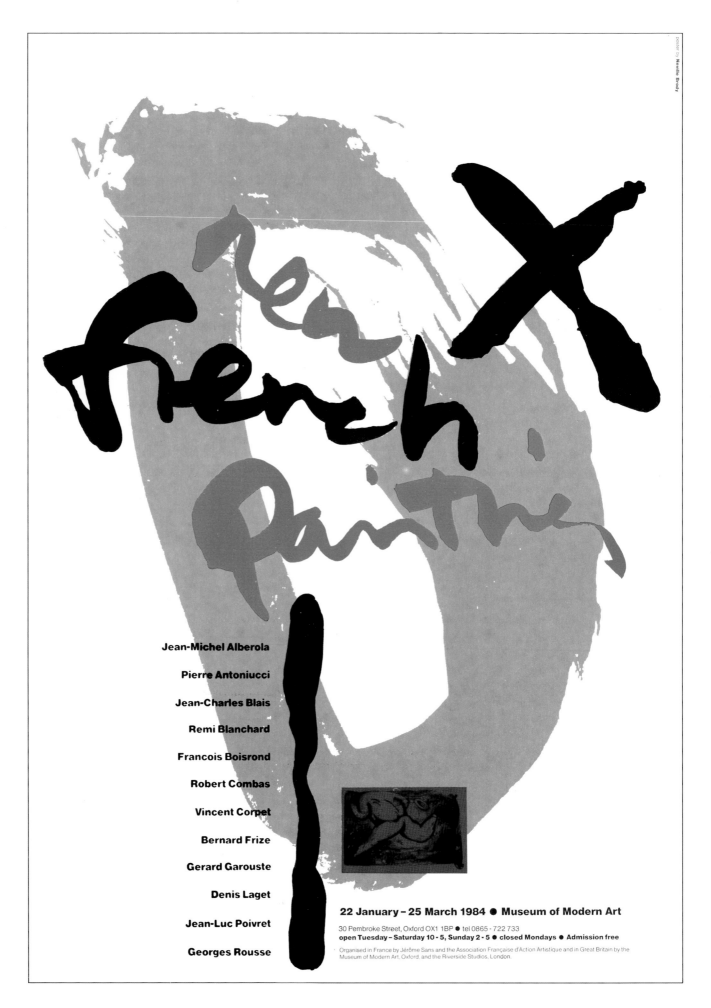

39. A2 poster for New French Painting exhibition at the Museum of Modern Art, Oxford, 1983
Brody ran into disagreement with the museum's curators over his decision to graphically express the feel of the exhibition, choosing not to illustrate directly the works on show.

Jean-Michel Alberola

Pierre Antoniucci

Jean-Charles Blais

Remi Blanchard

Francois Boisrond

Robert Combas

Vincent Corpet

Bernard Frize

Gerard Garouste

Denis Laget

Jean-Luc Poivret

Georges Rousse

22 January – 25 March 1984 ● Museum of Modern Art

30 Pembroke Street, Oxford OX1 1BP ● tel 0865 - 722 733
open Tuesday – Saturday 10 - 5, Sunday 2 - 5 ● closed Mondays ● Admission free

Organised in France by Jérôme Sans and the Association Française d'Action Artistique and in Great Britain by the Museum of Modern Art, Oxford, and the Riverside Studios, London.

**40-44. Catalogue and other material for
New French Painting exhibition, 1983**

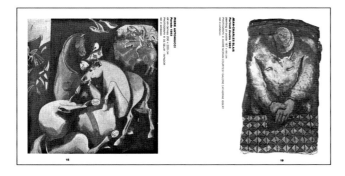

40. Catalogue cover
Typographic style based on brush marks,
printed in two colours on 275 gsm Dutch
greyboard.

41. The majority of images included in the
96-page catalogue were monochrome or
two-colour; its format was 140 X 150 mm.

42. The luxury of space allowed for each
artist to be allocated an individual showcase
of painting and text, the latter with line-
spacing justified to the same depth.

43/44. Invitation and newsletter cover

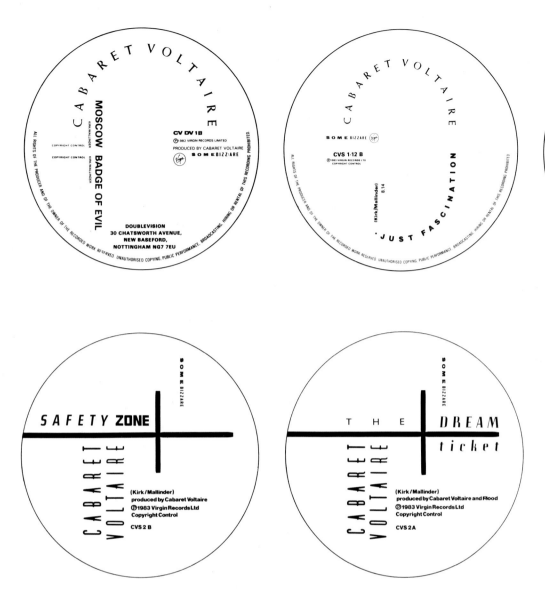

45. **Cabaret Voltaire record labels, Virgin Records, 1982 and 1983**
The design focused on typographic movement. Elements that had been used on the cover were combined with standard label information to create a self-contained unit.

46. **Z'ev video label, Fetish Records, 1981**

'Once you start with the realisation that, in a magazine, words are recognition factors, then letter-spacing becomes part of a modular system. Your structure is a sign system. The elements that dictate that system are signs, symbols and words. With *The Face* it was taken down to that basic modular level, and once you've done this, words can be used to do other things. They can be used to create lines of direction. To begin with, it was partly a reaction to the Seventies' habit of tight setting; with the information explosion, people reacted not by simplifying things, but by compressing them. People didn't condense the type, they simply condensed the space. With computer typesetting, you started to get an overlapping, where for instance on two lines of type the top part of a capital "A" would be touched by a lower case "g" above it. Or the last two letters in the word "Very". So with *The Face*, and the use of letter-spacing, I was in effect saying "Let's have a little more time to consider these things". I was trying to slow down the pace, to create breathing spaces, space to consider and think. It also made you notice the characteristics of an individual letter, and how that combined with others to make up a word. It introduced a sense of rhythm.

This is something that didn't really come to fruition until I started to hand-draw the headlines. The space, call it negative space if you like, is just as important as the positive space where the type falls. An editorial exists on many levels — it does not consist only of words. And any design colours the way in which you read the content. The typeface you use, its size, the way you space it, the position you choose — all these affect the way in which you read a piece.'

'*If you didn't know much about typography, what made you choose Helvetica and Futura for text setting?*'

'I used these typefaces when I felt that a sans-serif type expressed the sense of the subject matter. In geometric terms, Futura is unequalled in its purity, and Helvetica carries an elegant authority, but there are certain practical constraints which come through. Futura is usually unfavourable because of its small and uneconomical "x" height, few words to a line, whereas if you condense it slightly, it becomes much more even to the eye. Helvetica I chose in preference to Univers, which I find to be the coldest face ever designed — it's so mechanically pure in its intentions that it's still-born, it can't communicate any emotive quality whatsoever. It's a clever typeface, but so dry, so cold.
▶ *p. 35*

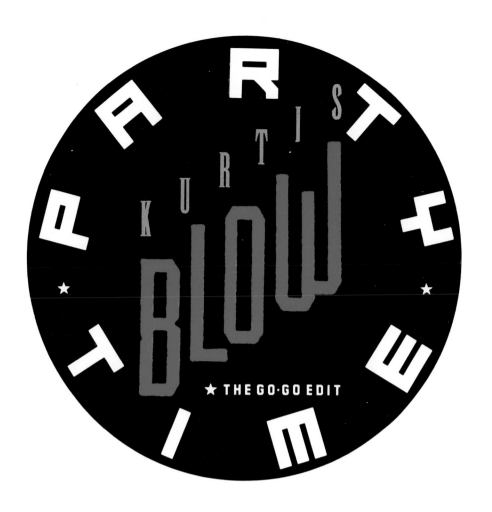

47/48. Original design and cover for Kurtis Blow, *Party Time*, Phonogram Records, 1985
The design sat on a white ground. The record company thought this version lacked the necessary immediacy for in-store display. Brody adapted the design to produce the final sleeve, shown below.

49. Back and front cover for *Fresh New Beats* compilation, Cool Tempo Records, 1986
The square upon which the design was placed had an overprinted spot varnish, creating a contrast between matt and gloss.

ABCDEFGHIJKLMN
OPQRSTUVWXYZ"
abcdefghijkllmn
opqrsttuvwxyz!

50/51/52/53. Typeface Two, designed for *The Face*, 1984, used from issue 50 onwards
Brody felt that there was no typeface at the time that suited the specific mood he sought for *The Face*. The geometric quality of the type was authoritarian, drawing a parallel between the social climate of the 1930s and the 1980s. This geometry also allowed for flexibility in use — which could be playful in order to undermine the type's assertive form. The type was used in various weights.

JAMES TRUMAN+USA

selling england's soul

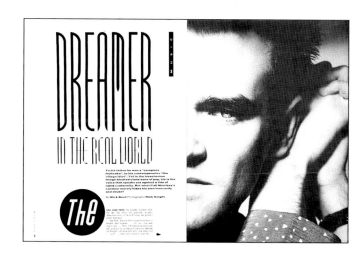

54. Typeface Four designed for *The Face*, 1985, used from issue 61 onwards
The type was designed for use at a large size, creating a dynamism on the page and allowing for an open use of white space. The typeface had an over-stated personality that highlighted the unusual step of drawing a typeface specifically for one magazine.

55. Morrissey spread, *The Face*, No. 61, May 1985
The relationship between headline, photograph bled into the centre of the page, and the opening word of the text, was exaggerated to contrast with the fine lines of the hand-drawn type.

56. **Punctuation symbols for** *The Face*
Directional symbols follow the text.

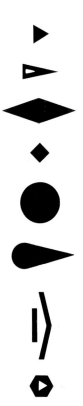

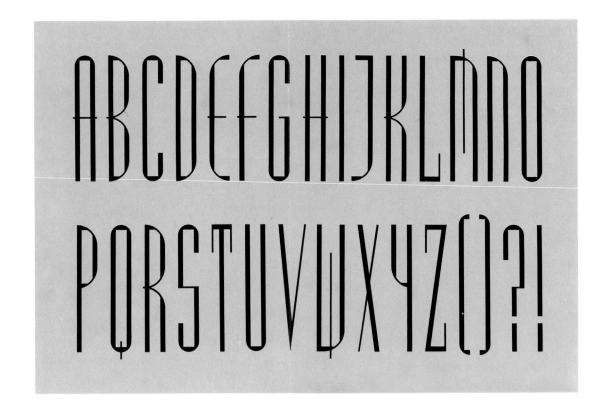

57. **Typeface Five, designed for** *The Face*,
1985, used from issue 61 onwards
The combination of thick and thin lines with a
geometric structure created a letterform that
conveyed a modern classicism. The type was
deliberately economical.

58. **Cameo spread,** *The Face*, **No. 65,**
September 1985
The photograph was used sideways and the
headline striking in spite of its size.

59. During this period, Brody frequently
used the extended lozenge shape as a
typographical device — shown here as the
credit on the above spread.

PROFILE **DAVE RIMMER** PHOTOGRAPHS **SHEILA ROCK**

60. **Typeface Three**, which immediately
followed the typeface shown in Fig. 50. The
type had built-in variables to give greater
flexibility for headlines.

A B C D E F G H I I
J K L M N O P Q R !
S T U V W X Y Z [?]

61/62/63. Typeface Six designed for *The Face*, 1986, used from issue 73 onwards
The typeface was designed to replace the Futura that had been used extensively throughout previous issues. It is based on a square and a circle, further developing the idea of using a geometric base. As with fig. 57, the type was drawn only in upper-case.

THE FACE

64. Logo for *The Face*, 1987
'The way *The Face* has been set up through its seven years has given a lot of freedom that wouldn't exist in a large publishing house. Quite simply, it could not have been called *The Face* if it had been published by a larger concern, because there is no way I could have explained to anyone else why I wanted to call it this. I just liked the combination of words. So many other decisions on design and editorial come about for the same reasons, what feels right, and they are made on the spot.' (Nick Logan, July 1987).

The original look Nick Logan had wanted for *The Face* was similar to European news magazines like *Paris Match* — simple, pictorial and direct. Phil Bicker's appointment as Art Director in Summer 1987 was a good time to update the magazine's front cover. Brody was commissioned to create a logo that suggested a more journalistic feel that could easily be adapted in line with the cover photograph. Having come up with a range of options, mostly italic, the best turned out to be the re-introduction of an earlier type design — shown below — a *Picture Post* for the Eighties.

A B C D E F G H I I
J K L M N O P Q R
S T U V W X Y Z ‼

65. Brody introduced the language of corporate logos and informational signs to a magazine layout, undermining and highlighting their everyday function by using them out of context. The magazine spread itself takes on a corporate identity.

66. Headline for Gil Evans feature, *The Face*, No.38, June 1983
A combination of Grotesque No.7 and No.9, this is one of the earliest designs where the letterform was abstracted. The weight change helps the balance of the vertically-placed headline.

67. Soca Pressure, *The Face*, No.60, April 1985
An emblematic motif used throughout the
feature—the hand-drawn letters were condensed
not by squashing the type but by cutting off each
outer edge.

**68. Headline for Tom Waits feature, *The
Face*, No.67, November 1985**
The type was drawn exclusively for the
headline—Brody wanted to further extend his
control over the magazine's typeforms.

**70. Frankie Goes To Hollywood, *The Face*,
No.56, December 1984**
Taken out of context, the individual
letterforms are hardly recognisable as such,
yet can be read in combination. A deliberate
exercise in kitsch—but not totally over the top.

**71. Headline for Billy MacKenzie feature,
The Face, No.60, April 1985**
The headline was placed in parentheses to
graphically 'phrase' its meaning. The type
has been cut away, yet the eye completes the
words.

**69. The Modern Jazz, *The Face*,
No.72, April 1986**
Whilst the type structure is broken
down to a more expressive form, the
words can still be read and the whole is
held within a modular system that
creates a further graphic unit.

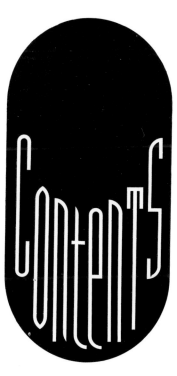

**72. Contents logo, *The Face*, No.62,
June 1985**
The type is forced to follow the shape
imposed upon it.

73. Style logo as it degenerated over four issues of *The Face*, Nos. 49, 51, 52, 53, May, July to September 1984
74. Style logo, now completely abstract, *The Face*, No.52, August 1984

'The Past is being plundered in Pop as elsewhere in order to construct a totality that is seamless, that cannot be broken. It is a characteristic of our age that there is little sense of community, of any *real* sense of history, as THE PRESENT is all that matters. Who needs yesterday's papers? In re-fashioning the past in our own image, in tailoring the past to our own preconceptions, the past is recuperated: instead of being a door OUT of our time, it merely leads to another airless room.

The Past is then turned into the most disposable of consumer commodities, and is thus dismissable: the lessons it can teach us are thought trivial, and are ignored amongst a pile of garbage.'
(Jon Savage, 'The Age of Plunder', *The Face*, No.33, January 1983).

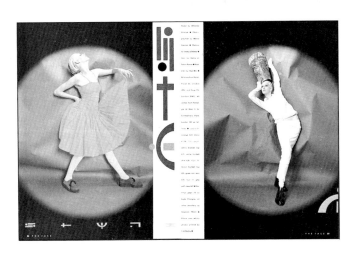

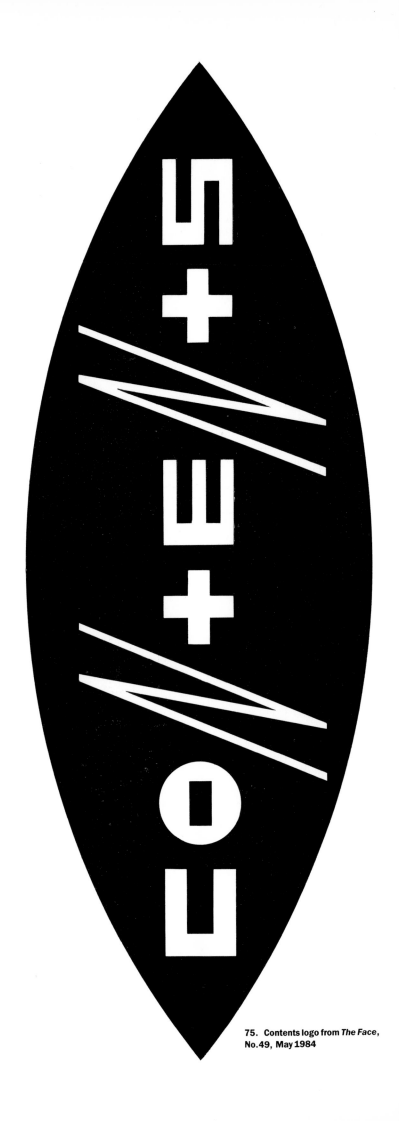

75. Contents logo from *The Face*, No.49, May 1984

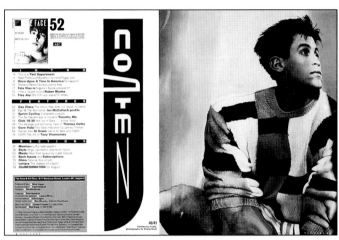

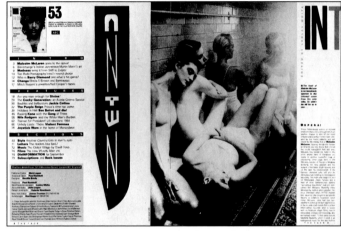

76/77/78/79/80/81. Contents pages from
***The Face*, Nos.50 to 55, 1984**

'With the steady breakdown of the Contents logo,
I was dealing with two ideas. First, the notion of
modular design based on a set of units that fit
together according to their use. Second, to
achieve a more organic design that changed over
a period of time. Over eight or nine issues, the
word 'Contents' was stripped down until it
became two marks — a way of pinpointing and
highlighting the recognition of words as opposed
to their readability. I was also questioning the
role of the Contents page in a magazine, and
more widely, visual coding as it applied to written
language.

'The same with the Style logos. Initially,
these too were drawn-up to look like corporate
symbols, but as they developed into abstract
marks, people could still read them as 'style' and
might not have even noticed that the word was no
longer made up of real letters.'

JERICHO BUGLE PRESENTS

THE BEAT BOX

EVERY THURSDAY 10 TILL 2
AT THE CAPE OF GOOD HOPE
· MAGDALEN ROUNDABOUT

THE JERICHO BUGLE PRESENTS THE

ARMAGEDDON ball

ANIMAL NIGHTLIFE
+ 2 SUPPORT BANDS · SHEWS DISCOTHEQUE
FRIDAY NOVEMBER 25TH 10.30 – 6.00
AT THE GRAVENHILL THEATRE, BICESTER
COACHES AVAILABLE

TICKETS · £16 (INCLUDES FREE WINE AND SPIRITS + CONTINENTAL BREAKFAST)
FROM · REBECCA NICOLSON · 14 NEWTON ROAD · OXFORD · TEL: 251072

82/83. *Opposite:* **Posters for Oxford University social events, 1984**

84. *Elephant Talk* **fanzine cover, 1984**
The image expressed the breakdown in human communication.

85. *The Face* **Turin party invitation, 1986**

86. **Magazine advert for Torchsong, 1984**
Composed entirely of type, the background is formed by text reproduced out of focus.

Helvetica is much warmer, and is more intricate. I'd previously rejected it totally because it was a typeface of the Seventies, but that hard, ranged-left, tight-spaced unemotional use didn't succeed then because Helvetica does have character to it. The difference between the "K" in Helvetica and Univers bears this out.

All along the line, I've tried to use typefaces that have gone against the grain of contemporary fashion; in a lot of cases, this is Univers 49, wide-spaced, which I find despicable — but I must admit to having used it myself when I was less aware of typographic form. It's clumsy, really non-emotive. It's the same with Century Schoolbook. Century and Univers are, in their different ways, supposedly the ultimate in pure type, which of course is another fiction; but I've returned to the use of Helvetica, particularly with *Arena*, because part of the legacy from *The Face* and from Malcolm Garrett's work is to create a desperate wild style without rhyme or reason where designers throw something at a wall, using devices not because they understand them but because someone else has thrown something at a wall. It's become an extremely mannered use of type.

I chose Garamond for body text in *The Face* and *Arena* because it has a warmth to it, a grace to the formation and flow of the letters; and it's very easy to read, which is something I don't find with Century and Univers. Although Garamond is traditionally a book-face, we're using it nevertheless in a magazine format.

Times is a typeface I hate. I've always hated Times, but I often reverted to it because in many instances it provided the only solution. It was designed for newspaper use, and in certain contexts there is no other typeface that fits the bill. Times was designed for a modern format, so we used it for a lot of the body copy in *The Face*, and while it was originally designed for letterpress printing, it adapts to offset litho far better than any of the other traditional typefaces. But it's as ugly as hell, and when you look at a piece of work set in Times, you see nothing but a piece of work set in Times. Once again, it has a horrible Seventies' dryness about it. It's not passive, though — only in people's reactions to it, so if anything it's passive in the wrong way. Garamond communicates a greater energy than the sum of the words on the page. Times doesn't.

I would like to use Baskerville more, but Baskerville shares the same problem as Futura — a very small "x" height, which is difficult to print. As a letterpress typeface, it hasn't adapted successfully to the unreliability of much modern printing.

I dislike the ITC (International Type Corporation) cuts of typefaces, which has been one response to the problem of printability. Really, I don't know what they think they're doing — in a way, it's an attempt to create an American typographic tradition out of European type. The ITC faces have a very Seventies' look, too, and if you use them large, this use colours what you are trying to

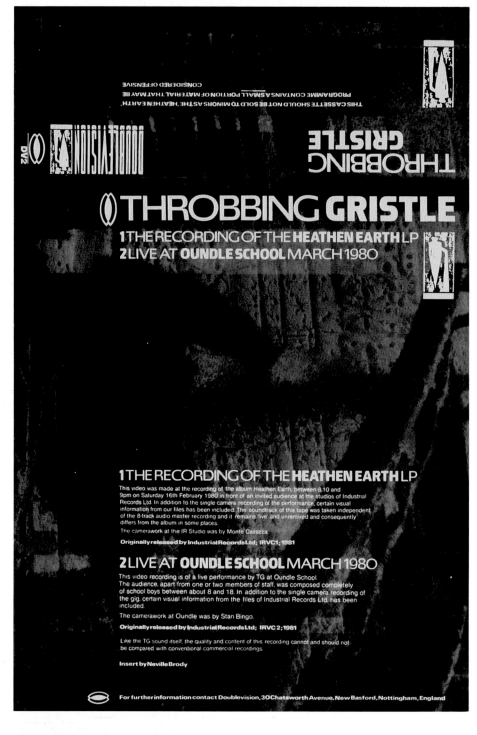

'We're not interested in information, we're not interested in music as such. And we believe that the whole battlefield, if there is one in the human situation, is about information.'
(Throbbing Gristle, quoted in *Industrial Culture Handbook*, Re-Search Publications, 1983).

87/88. Throbbing Gristle video inlay-card, Doublevision, 1983
Informational typography in the style of a company training video, overlaid on distressed clay-relief images, and schoolchildren.

89. Poster for Throbbing Gristle video, 1983

communicate so completely that it overrides your intentions. ITC faces don't have the kind of anonymity that a good colour has in painting. If you use one, then what you're really doing is revealing a part of the painting that you haven't created.

There's much reasoning to do with historical use, conventional use and practical use of typography. Certain typefaces I will use because of their historical context and the way that I react personally to an undercurrent, so with *Arena* I returned to Helvetica because it had preceded this age of typographic mannerism, this lunacy where people really don't understand what they're doing. They know what they want to signify, but they don't understand the grammar of what they're doing. It's got out of hand. It's reached the point where certain High Street shops are commissioning designs in the full knowledge that in two years they'll have to redesign. This is now a matter of policy, so what it says is irrelevant — the signification is all important, and its suggestion that "we belong" or, rather, that your money belongs with us. It's a desperate con, just another advertising game. Again, advertising has stolen valid typographic devices, ripped the reasoning out, and used them as surface style by implying that it understands a common language. But is this a common language? No it happens to be shared by their target audience. They're talking, but it's empty words, and now that the styles of "Youth Culture" permeate everywhere, this common language is projected at people whose individual experience is years ahead of its faked energy. Language is supposed to be organic — the signification in advertising results in a kind of claustrophobia, an ever-tightening circle into which anything can be absorbed; despite devices like letter-spacing, it gives no space to the viewer. So with the choice of Helvetica, I'm simply saying "STOP".

There are no rules being broken at the moment — everything has broken down, the traditions and the established order have been challenged by Punk and no-one has been rebuilding. With that, and the information explosion that we're still living through, I can't see the situation being resolved at least until the end of this century. I'm talking about real solutions, not transient ones. Yet because of the hunger and greed of the advertising industry, they have to claim temporary measures and examples as being "permanent truths" of current society. In doing so, they abduct the viewer. It's all premature — wide-spaced type was, for me, a way of revealing the problem. It's not the solution. We don't know what the solution looks like — we're feeling our way towards it as we're discovering and challenging the problems. However, the people in control who have this need for a common language are assuming it to be the end. For me, Helvetica is like going up a sharp cliff and finding a bench to sit on for a while to check the lie of the land. It's not pastiche. It's not being used as nostalgia. It is used as a form of solidifying, saying "That's one period of exploration over in typography — let's look at what we've done before making the next move." It's also a return to a more basic level of pure information. Helvetica does colour the way that information

90/91. Cabaret Voltaire video inlay-card, Doublevision, 1983
Doublevision is an independent video and record outlet set up by Cabaret Voltaire. The double eye symbol gave the company a corporate identity which acted as both pivot and punctuation for the rest of the design. The cooling tower symbol appeared at the beginning of all their videos, and can be seen outside their Western Works recording studios in Sheffield.

T H E · S O U N D · O F · W A S H I N G T O N · D · C

71 MINUTES OF **REDDS + THE BOYS** ● **PETWORTH** ● **SHADY GROOVE**
2 LP-SET OR DOUBLE-PLAY CASSETTE FOR THE PRICE OF ONE
DOUBLE-LP ● BOMB I / DOUBLE-PLAY Mc ● KBOMB I ● ORDER FROM POLYGRAM: 01 590-6044

**92/94. Record cover for Go-Go, *The Sound
of Washington, D.C.*, London Records, 1985**
In the absence of any photographs, Brody
chose to typographically reflect the language
of American highway signs.

93. Press advert for Go-Go compilation, 1985

95. Artists Against Apartheid logo, 1986
A direct symbol to convey racial segregation.

is perceived, there's no way of avoiding this, but it is more "settled" than anything else.'

'Did you ever use handwriting in The Face*?'*

'It was something that I was loathe to do, because there was a trend at the time – whenever somebody wanted something to look "loose", "modern" and fashionable, they'd use a handwritten headline. However, I do use a script face in *Arena* for the credits on each individual feature as a means of softening the informational quality of the design. In the early period of *The Face*, I tended to crudely hand-render headlines, but this was a reaction to the slickness of magazine design at that time.

In the short term, I definitely think we're heading towards more loosely and crudely designed types, more personalised, more earthy and more basic.'

'Like restaurant menus?!'

'No, they're too contrived. And you mustn't confuse handwriting with something that is hand-drawn. I know what you mean, but those menus are an attempt to signify either friendliness or the fact that the restaurant is a traditional one. Distant utopias. It's also a class distance, it's offering the promise that for a short period of time you can be "one of us", even if the "us" is never actually stated. And by writing a menu by hand rather than getting it typeset, you're suggesting that the chef will take great personal care in preparing the food. It seems that if you want to communicate something that's thought to be "natural", then you immediately use handwriting. It's a way of signifying something soft. Nature isn't like that.'

96/97/98. Red Wedge logos, 1985

'From its outset, we realised that if Red Wedge was going to have any chance of representing a new spirit on the left and appealing to young people, its graphic presentation had to be as sharp as anything in the commercial sector. The name itself was taken from an El Lissitsky 1920s abstract painting – so it followed that the logo should have a strong Constructivist element, though without wearing a Rodchenko uniform. Neville's logo served as an illustration in itself and as a corporate stamp for merchandising.' (Neil Spencer, founder member of Red Wedge).

'What do you mean by "organic typography"?'

'Type is seen as being extra-territorial, but it's not; type is used to express an inner feeling and reaction; it has to be. It's not a natural phenomenon, it symbolises a thought process. It's organic in its basis, it's man-created. On the other hand, if you believe in the purity of type forms, you're also believing in a fallacy. It's a flexible means of expression that man should have control over. You should be able to adapt the appearance of type to suit your own purpose. Too many people believe in the unshakable purity and truth of type. If, say, Baskerville doesn't quite work, then you should modify its letters. Traditionalists would say "that's sacrilege", because typographic training is based around a belief in the purity of the typeforms you're using. Rules created by another generation for a different social order have to be modified for the present. With the use of the word "organic", I wanted to get across the idea that communication is ever-evolving and ever-changing. With *The Face*, I was stripping things right down, thereby highlighting the recognition of words. The Contents logo started off with hand-drawn and recognisable letters, but it ended up as abstract shapes that could still be read as the word itself.'

'If *The Face* was about *signification*, as you say, then it should have been no surprise that it — and your own work — was so widely imitated.'

'The thing is, *The Face* set up a strange tradition for itself. For the first time, here was a magazine which people expected to change in style every week. The only way if could have challenged itself was by remaining the same. As soon as that becomes a tradition, change again. And by the time that the change once again becomes a tradition, the magazine should have folded. There has to be a constant process of self-challenge.

What I was doing was over-highlighting the fact that things can and do change constantly — even with what I was stating, there are no truths. There were always other alternatives to what was being done. On the Eno feature in *The Face* (fig.310), I used what I thought was possibly the most ugly typeface in the world, I think it was Jackson, trying to force myself into new challenges — to use it in a way that was aesthetically acceptable.'

'How much of the hand-drawn quality of your type for *The Face* do you think was transmitted to the reader?'

'That wasn't the point to begin with — initially, I was angry that people were immediately copying what I was doing: it was easy to find the typefaces that we were using, and to modify them in the way that we were. People used to ring up the office and ask "What was the typeface you used on such and such a page?". I wanted to produce something that others would find difficult to mimic.

The second point was that I did want to start working directly with my hands again. We xeroxed the typeface, and then stuck the letters together on a line, which meant that there was even more control than before. During my last year with *The Face*, this culminated in every single headline in the magazine being hand-drawn for its specific use. I don't think we could have gone any further than that. We could have gone crazy with them, but there wouldn't have been any point. Look at the Frankie headline (fig.70).'

'Do you ever worry about small blemishes in your drawing-up of a letterform?'

'I feel intimidated by major ones. Where I think *The Face* was most successful is that we always paid a lot of attention to our detailing — it wasn't just a gestural "Let's throw the headline down and hope that the rest sorts itself out".

But even by going through the printing process, whatever you've drawn is going to undergo some degradation. When I first started hand-drawing type, there was a lot I didn't know. I would join curves to lines, instead of vice-versa. Small details annoy me, but the perfection of the flow is the most important thing. Sometimes the human touch is even better with the mistakes.'

'Have you ever seen a use of your hand-drawn type by someone else that you've liked?'

'No, I can't say that I have. I wish I could. It's signification again. If other people understood why, they wouldn't be using my typeface, they'd be drawing their own.'

99. CND logo proposals, 1985
Some of the CND leadership were keen to update the organisation's image and to increase its sense of relevance to a new generation. Sadly, the conservative elements within the leadership prevailed and the proposals were resisted. These represent a starting point to show what can be done without losing the strength of the original logo. One critic, however, suggested that the whole idea was akin to commissioning Andy Warhol to help redesign the Soviet Flag.

NEW SOCIALIST NO 38 MAY 1986 **90p/$3**

NEW SOCIALIST

STYLE WARS

DAVID EDGAR VERSUS
ROBERT ELMS

JUNE JORDAN: ISRAEL'S UNHOLY ALLIANCE
FEMINISM AND **CLASS POLITICS**

FALL-OUT OVER LIBYA

100. Cover of *New Socialist*, May 1986

103. *New Socialist* **letterhead**

Brody was asked to redesign the Labour Party's monthly magazine, *New Socialist*, in 1986. The commission was for a total reappraisal of the magazine's visual identity that included all its other printed matter, the job involving similar design criteria to those for corporate identity symbols. The brief was to extend the appeal of the magazine and its political content beyond Labour Party faithfuls so as to reach a wider and younger audience. The typographic style had to convey the idea that politics is an area that affects everyday life; it had to be bold and classical, stating an extreme modernity alongside established tradition. To achieve this, Brody contrasted geometrically-based hand-drawn type, used at a large size, with wide-spaced Bodoni type.

The first cover (opposite) intended a bold over-statement in which the new logo became the cover illustration, announcing the momentum of the content.

For the stationery (below right), a deeper red was used as the second colour (see pp. 130-132), rather than the customary scarlet associated with the politics of the Left.

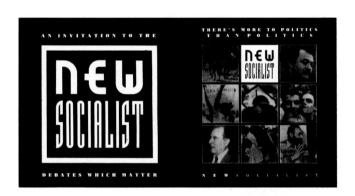

101/102. *New Socialist* **promotional literature**

104/105/106. Hyper Hyper clothes market, publicity campaign, 1984

HYPER HYPER ✦ 26-40 KENSINGTON HIGH STREET ●

LONDON W8 ☎ TEL : 0 1 9 3 7 6 9 6 6 / 6 4

OPENING HOURS 🕐 MON-SAT 10AM-6PM ● THURS 10AM-7PM

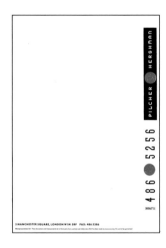

107. Estate agent's property particulars form, Pilcher Hershman, 1987
108. Estate agent's board, Pilcher Hershman, 1987
Pilcher Hershman took the unusual step of commissioning Brody to come up with a sale board design that was more architecturally direct. The premise was that 'For Sale' signs should not even exist: here is an example of a recurrent dilemma. Brody designed a typeface exclusively for this brief, where the normal commercial imperative, that of attracting the eye from a distance, was directed away from the size of the words themselves.

109. Letterhead for Panny Charrington, 1982
Based on images produced by Panny
Charrington, the design was printed on a
grey-fleck paper stock, with the typographic
information loosely hand-rendered.

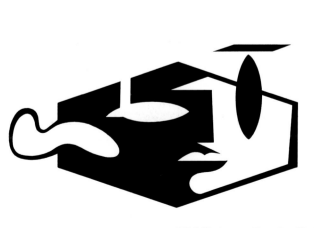

**110/111. Logo and letterhead for Second
International Video Festival, 1982**

112. Press release for Dont Flex, video production company, 1982
The image combines the heads of a tiger and a cow. An anti-press release press release, with an design that undermines the readability of any subsequently-typed information. The main typeface was enlarged from an IBM golfball typewriter, Copperplate Gothic, partly because photo-typesetting was beyond the budget.

DONTFLEX
INTERNATIONAL
PRESSRELEASE
CONTACT 01-671 1518

27/29 BLENHEIM GARDENS, LONDON SW2 5EV.

113/114/115. Logos and letterhead for Dont Flex
The original logo was developed as an expression of strength through pain. The hammer and the nail replaced the 'D' and 'X' of Dont Flex.

DONT FLEX PRODUCTIONS LTD
27/29 BLENHEIM GARDENS LONDON SW2 5EU
TELEPHONE 01-671 1518   VAT 340 1351 11

DONTFLEX

116. Domestic press release for Dont Flex
The area for typing information onto the page was severely restricted, and would be barely visible. The dominant crab motif was constructed from a variety of abstract marks, with other design elements reduced to signposting. It was printed on a texture-embossed grey paper.

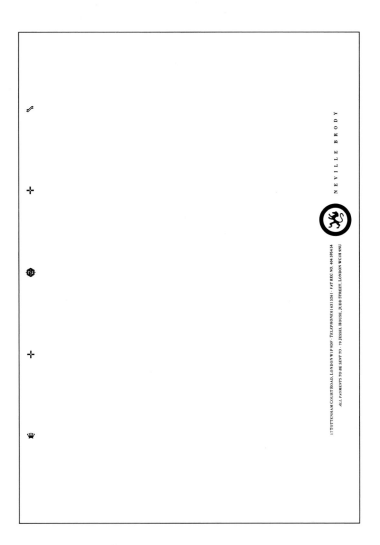

117/118/119. Personal stationery and monogram, 1987
A 6-point motif depicting a cockerel was greatly enlarged and used in conjunction with industrial and heraldic marks. These denoted typing and folding instructions. The monogram was designed to suggest a practical use – a tool rather than a totem.

S U B : C O U T U R E

NORTH'WING

S U B : C O U T U R E

FURTHER INFORMATION CONTACT
RACHEL O'NEIL AT ZED ON 01 251 2405
NORTH WING 398 ST JOHNS STREET, LONDON EC1.
TELEPHONE 01 278 6473

BROCHURE DESIGNED BY NEVILLE BRODY
ILLUSTRATIONS BY CHRISTOPHER BRUCE

SHAPE

NORTH'WING

PROPOSALS FOR 'Sub-Couture' – Winter 87 – shape and texture – wools and corduroy – charcoals and cinnamon – snug, melton, 'soldier boy' jackets – rippling petal skirts, cropped, corolla dresses – soft needle-cord shirts – creamy, springy jerseys – 'North Wing'

120/121/122. Fashion show brochure and insert for North Wing, 1987
Unlike the accepted treatment given to fashion brochures, North Wing wanted something that suggested irreverence, the exploration of new ideas, and a confident approach to clothes design. The invitation (below right), together with the drawings of the garments, were inserted into the outer folder.

123. Logo development for North Wing, 1987
The basic logo was taken to a more chaotic conclusion, with the idea that it would constantly evolve.

INVITATION **N** orthwing invite you to come and see their **Winter '87**

'sub-couture' collection at the **Basil Street Hotel**, 8 Basil Street, SW3 – just off Sloane Street,

Ask for **suite number 246.** From the

14th to the 17th March, 10am – 8pm. **14 – 17**

We would be delighted to meet you and show you our samples and video.

RSVP

Contact Rachel O'Neil, at ZED Agency . 01-251 2405 or

North Wing, on 01-278 6473 Please bring ticket with you.

NORTH'WING

m o n o t y p e

TYPOGRAPHY

c a n t o r i a

Cantoria is an exciting new face from Monotype's Ron Carpenter which follows in the tradition of earlier Monotype faces such as *Della Robbia* (1902) and *Canterbury* (1915).

Cantoria, however, has a clear identity of its own, with the bolder weights retaining the individuality of character which can sometimes be lost as weights increase.

Cantoria has been created as a large family of romans and *italics* and this broad choice of lights **to *bolds* makes it an ideal face for advertising or magazine work.**

avanti

COMPILED BY STEVE TAYLOR, MICHAEL WATTS

STUDIO PHOTOGRAPHY DAVIES & STARR

STRONGER **VODKAS**... NEW
LOOK **BETTING SHOPS**...
MATTHEW HILTON'S **TUBULAR
FURNITURE**... **PAUL SMITH**
IN PARIS... THE MICRO-**CAMERA**
CHUNKY TYROLEAN FOOTWEAR...
SWISS ARMY KNIVES... THE
ELECTRONIC **ORGANISER**...

ARENA **10** WINTER

124. *Opposite:* **Cover for type prospectus, Monotype, 1986**
The brief was to produce a design that explored and expressed the specific qualities of a new typeface that Monotype was introducing for computer typesetting machines.

125. Opening page to the 'Avanti' section, *Arena*, No.1, Winter 1986
The typeface used for the main heading was later developed as a complete fount, below, and then applied to other sections of the magazine. In lower-case only, this condensed type emphasised the use of thick and thin to evoke a modern classicism. The structure is less geometrically based than previous typefaces designed by Brody, relying more upon an elliptical format. The short ascenders and descenders on the letters create a large 'x' height, allowing for a greater readability at a small point size.

abcdefghijklmnopqrstuvwxyzæœ!?()

MUSIC:FETISH RECORDS

New Rose, released in 1977 by one of the leading Punk groups of the time, The Damned, was an early example of a picture sleeve crucial in combating the common belief — which Punk was trying to break down — that performers' personalities were more important than their music. At this time, the ideas behind a record were thought to be the main priority; records would be released with picture sleeves that gave the opportunity for experimentation in design whereby it could express the music by using sources other than photographs of the group. This change provided the catalyst for a generation of new designers, of whom Barney Bubbles, Malcolm Garrett, Al McDowell, Chris Morton, Jamie Reid and Peter Saville are just a few. Their work revitalised the assumptions underlying record sleeve design, introducing a host of new graphic possibilities that were international in their effect, and not only on areas that influenced record packaging. Here was proof that design could become a lateral force, whilst staying true to the spirit of the recordings, its content. Moreover, it was a commercial success that resuscitated the old as well as introduced the new.

It did not take long, therefore, for major record companies to follow this initiative; the cover had always been a part of any record's commercial potential, but it had been some time, except in isolated instances during the early 1970s when a design group such as Hipgnosis had challenged the form, since record covers had really captured the popular imagination — probably not since The Beatles' *Sgt. Pepper* in 1967. Work done by Roger Dean for the group Yes cannot really be counted in this category, for although his cover design posters adorned many bedroom walls in 1973, their content was no more challenging than an airbrushed greetings card. Record companies, however, still failed to pick up on this potential; once it was realised that more attention paid to cover design would pay off commercially, the picture sleeve became a crucial promotional device. The subsequent wave of picture discs and coloured vinyl has only recently been abated by the more lucrative promise of compact discs. In 1979, however, the record business offered designers a fair degree of free expression. Independent record companies had achieved a commercial success disproportionate to their means, which caused new companies to be formed, and the older ones to try to emulate the majors. For the independent record sector as a whole, this marks the point at which the creative impetus gives way to divisive commercialism; for others, the possibilities afforded by the music at the time (a glorious twilight) could be developed before financial and distributive constraints made things totally unworkable. At opposite ends of this spectrum were Stiff Records and Fetish Records.

Whilst working at Stiff, Neville Brody witnessed the way in which the commercial aspirations of the company undermined its creative potential. The promotional strategies of the music business did not sit comfortably with the manipulative process that the music and its imagery was trying to reveal. One of Stiff

Records' early and most infectious slogans was 'Undertakers to the Music Business', and as far as the independent initiative was concerned, the company stayed true to its rhetoric.

It is a constant dilemma with any independent initiative to balance the need for commercial success — and thereby both survival and the extension of popularity beyond simply preaching to the converted — with the 'purity' of the ideas. In the record business, this reached an apogee with Malcolm McLaren and Jamie Reid's last work with the Sex Pistols, *The Great Rock 'n' Roll Swindle*, where (amongst other ringmaster cracks of the whip) the Great Train Robber Ronnie Biggs was wheeled on to sing with the boys — 'Cosh the Driver' said the posters for the song 'No-one Is Innocent', which needless to say caused outrage. And as sure as death and taxes, money was the ultimate victor of this episode, as the group's subsequent split became embroiled in litigation.

In 1981, Brody became art director for Fetish Records, an independent label that gave him the chance to continue experimentation and to consolidate the ideas he had been working on while at college.

'Stiff taught me a lot about the workings of the music business, but I wasn't getting the chance to develop the ideas I

FETISH RECORDS

wanted to pursue. They had good intentions, but I knew that there were more interesting avenues to explore. I started working with Fetish Records at a time when I was living in a squat in Covent Garden with Tom Heslop, who was the lead singer in 23 Skidoo. We were both so broke that we used to work in the kitchens of Peppermint Park, a restaurant near Leicester Square. We used to do the washing-up to tapes of Rock 'n' Roll.

'Much of our free time revolved around the old Scala Cinema building in Tottenham Street (now the offices of Channel 4 TV). Here you could often see a group like Throbbing Gristle, playing on the same bill as films, and with the added bonus that the bar there had a good jukebox. Tom, myself and the others from 23 Skidoo used to frequent the place, and on one such occasion we

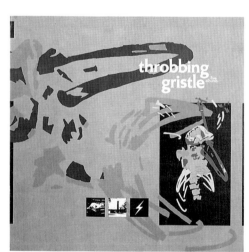

126. Throbbing Gristle, *Five Albums*, Fetish Records, 1982
'Rod Pearce kept up his contact with Industrial Records, and it was always Genesis P-Orridge's dream to put out a boxed set of Throbbing Gristle releases. There was a badge, a booklet, all in an nicely printed box — it was quite ironic that such outsiders should so effectively release an apparently coffee-table product. The main cover image was drawn by Laurence Dupré, and I then abstracted it further; she had previously been designing camouflage clothing for the group. The type was mock serious: we thought the image to be quite dangerous, but I don't know if it's worn the test of time. The project was an important one for Fetish to do. It sold well.'

127/128. *Opposite:* **Postcard and sticker for Fetish Records, 1981**
'We were conscious of what the other independent record companies were doing, and this was intended to be totally unfashionable, almost a caricature. The allusions to totem poles and to ritual were loose and crudely drawn. On the postcard, there is a reference to every band that was working with Fetish — record buying being ritualistic in itself. It was very tongue-in-cheek: The Bongos, for example, and little jokes like The Bush Tetras constantly on the phone because they came from New York and didn't visit London very often.'

129/130.   LP cover and sticker for the group 8 Eyed Spy, Fetish Records, 1981
'Al McDowell had introduced me to the work of the French film poster artists of the 1950s, which inspired the contrasts I was looking for. The cover is obviously in this cheap, pulp-detective style, but the agent is Asian, not Western. The '8 Eyed Spy' logo was developed from Japanese corporate symbols of the Forties and Fifties, and the 'Eyed' of the group's name was the first time I had ever drawn any type by hand for use on a cover. I completed the painting in two days (after spending three months on the verge of a nervous breakdown while working on the painting for a Slits album). I wanted it to be bold, crude and over-simplistic, to somehow illustrate the garageland feel of the band and of New York.'

53

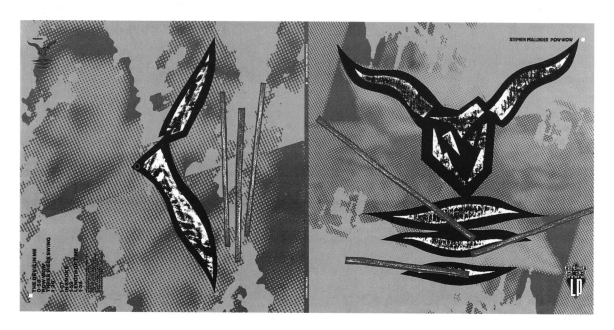

131. 8 Eyed Spy. 'Diddy Wah Diddy', Fetish Records 1982

'The sleeve was totally opposite to the music, but shared its sensibility — "Diddy Wah Diddy", the loss of human expression. The design is very macabre, where the markings were combined from a whole set of abstract ones that I'd made, with a painted background to solidify the mask-like face on the front and the skeletal image on the back. The result was grotesque — Fetish sleeves worked partly because they were entertaining'.

132. Z'ev, 'Wipe Out/Element L', Fetish Records, 1982

'The two colours, fluorescent orange and black, allude to a very modern scheme — what you would use for sale boards and 'go faster' signs. There is little hope on this sleeve — the shapes are undefeatable. The type was inspired by Futurist typography, and through the three-dimensional depth to the sleeve, I wanted to depict a disturbing world. Z'ev's version of 'Wipe Out' was quite apocalyptic.'

133. Stephen Mallinder, *Pow Wow*, Fetish Records 1983, re-issued by Doublevision, 1986

'This sleeve was about human ritual and human slaughter. In the media world of newscasters and advertisers everybody becomes a viewer; conditioned to regard other people's sufferings as no more than a form of entertainment. The bullring is a metaphor for this.'

134/135. *Opposite:* The Bongos, *Time and the River*, Fetish Records, 1982

'This design was inspired by photographs I had seen in the magazine *Soviet Union*, which presented the human image in a warm and dynamic form. This cover was optimistic and hopeful. *Time and the River* is about life, and the lust for life. The cover is a celebration, with soft colours, blue and green, the colours of the sea. I think the spirituality of this sleeve is more effective than on anything else I designed for Fetish, but it's questioned by the very bold star symbol on the reverse — a contrast between inner harmony and represented hope; it relates to different kinds of aspiration. There is no typesetting at all on the cover, the lettering being hand-rendered.'

THE BONGOS

time and the river

fetish 12"33 mini LP

'The musicians on Fetish were also totally open to the idea of me working under my own steam; there has been such a shift in this respect — most groups now take a much bigger hand in design, which does not necessarily make for a better cover. Furthermore, the time I was given to work on any one sleeve did vary, but it was always much longer than I ever get now. I would spend up to 70% of this period experimenting, constantly trying to push new ideas and techniques, notably on the PMT machine. Almost always, there was only a two-colour print possibility for the sleeves, so I quickly had to learn how to exploit this limitation. Everything would be proofed, but we could never afford the luxury of making many changes; we really had to know what we were aiming for from the start. There was a lot of tint-laying that sometimes did not produce the results intended, but I liked such surprises. I had learned from Al McDowell and Barney Bubbles that some mistakes can prove to be a boon.'

136. Bush Tetras, 'Das Ah Riot/ Boom', Fetish Records, 1981
'Again, everything here is done by hand, though it was all about the notion of texture — a very conscious exercise in total packaging, where the labels were the same as the cover image. The lizard is meant to provide an element of humour: the clearly man-made lines across the whole cover create a sense of the modern urban jungle.'

137. The Bongos, 'Zebra Club', Fetish Records, 1981
'This sleeve reiterated many of the ideas that went into *Pow Wow* (fig. 133). 'Zebra Club' was about levels of perception, so instead of using a zebra, I used a tiger — an animal that eats both zebras and humans. Making a point about superficiality, 'Zebra Club' is about dressing up, it's about surface levels, but the zebra is also a classic symbol used to refer to 'the double', the world of opposites. Men hunt tigers, and the sword of Zoro is slashed through the tiger's face. The real zebra has become background texture, wallpaper. It's about the sacrifice of human potential.'

138. Clock DVA, '4 Hours', Fetish Records, 1981
' "This could be New York, this could be London, I don't care anymore" — the song was about the modern living nightmare, and the loss of innocence. It's about desire, frustration and self-imposed limitations. The clock on the cover of *Thirst* (fig. 141) shows the time at 2, and on this one it's at 4.'

139. Bush Tetras, T-shirt design, 1981

140. Bush Tetras, label for 'Das Ah Riot', Fetish Records, 1981

came up with the idea for doing the sleeve for their first single for Fetish. This is where I met Rod Pearce, the head of Fetish Records, and luckily we got on like a house on fire.

'Fetish gave me total freedom, within the obvious limitations of its budget. From the start, Rod was prepared to let me get on with the job, and he always understood that my aim was to work in parallel with the music, and not simply to advertise it. The last thing he wanted was a picture of the band on the cover.

'With independent record companies like Industrial, and then Fast and Factory — all of whom had been highly influential — the dominant theme of their sleeves was to present an anti-conglomerate line through a parody of their own corporate image. Industrial Records was the most successful at this because their main group, Throbbing Gristle, used images of a real environment — Tesco supermarkets, tower-blocks and Ministry of Defence buildings — rather than try to subvert the stylistic conventions of corporate graphics. I'm sure than many people in 1988 consider Fetish as "one of the better independents" of its time, nevertheless thinking that it was no different from the general scene. This was not the case. At Fetish, we didn't want to create another mock-industrial empire; the identity of the label was based on a much more primitive sense of ritual than "the product". We

wanted to create something that wasn't self-referential but much earthier.

'My work for Fetish came out of a gut reaction to its music, and the situation it was being published in. I wanted to force the record buyer into a state of consideration — a gut reaction to my initial gut reaction. We never wanted to present things on a plate, but the dominant themes of my design were to open gateways that had been shut through fear, and to point to the loss of human identity and dignity within our immediate environment. A lot of the work represents a reaction to the commercial marketplace where the human form has become plastic. The sleeves are quite violent, but this is controlled by the medium. They all revolve around my intention to reintroduce human markings into commercial art. The real misery of people in modern Western society is that, through false representation in the media, you are conditioned to believe that either you are that representation, or that you should aspire to it. The reality and the advertisers' ideal are interchangeable, and what happens is that you literally miss out the middle man, the soul, the spirit and the vulnerability that are in all of us. But once you interpret this and try to give it a box, you weaken the motivation. The only way to understand is by looking, and then engaging.'

141/142. Clock DVA, *Thirst*, Fetish Records, 1981
'The sleeve is founded on three elements; the music, the writing by Genesis P-Orridge on the back, and the image itself. I had done a drawing that was not much bigger than a postage stamp, photocopied it and drawn over it once more, then enlarged it to the size of the cover. I wanted to attempt a different treatment on the theme of alienation, and treated the job as if it were a painting rather than an LP cover. If you look at it only from a painterly point of view, it *is* naive, but this I contrasted with the back cover which had to look professional and orderly; in this way people would not immediately think "this is just an independent cover for an independent label" and dismiss it on those terms. I remember at the time that I had difficulties placing the type, and a friend, Chris Pring, said "Look at it as you would do buildings and think of a factory". This was a key point in my understanding of design — that it is based on the most rudimentary of architectural principles, and that people react to it out of basic physical considerations. A sense of gravity is crucial.'

THE LAST TESTAMENT

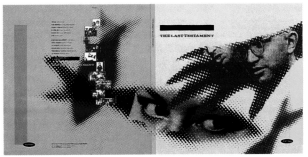

143/144. Various Artists, *The Last Testament*, Fetish Records, 1983
'This is a sad sleeve. It's really about the death of the whole independent record movement, where, for all your innocent enthusiasm, there is little hope. You can be swimming free, but there will always be somebody who comes along to try to exploit and control that freedom. If one struggle is between the head and the heart, ours was between major companies and independents. This was a sampler album of all the acts that Fetish had worked with, and it was the only other opportunity I had to use four-colour process (the first had been with the boxed set). Really, it's not even about losing your innocence — you're fished out and eaten before you get to reach that point. It's about the destructiveness of cynicism, but it also reflected the demise of Fetish Records at this point. The whole independent record system had imploded due to a mixture of greed, lack of conviction, and inefficiency — and took Fetish with it.'

CABARET VOLTAIRE

The group Cabaret Voltaire started out in 1973, the outcome of Richard Kirk, Stephen Mallinder and Chris Watson's experiments with sounds and tape recorders in Watson's loft. Sharing a common interest in cut-up and provocation with Throbbing Gristle and Industrial Records, Cabaret Voltaire soon became the principal exponents of a highly influential technique of combining film and video with their experimental music — their propaganda war against *the* propaganda war. After coming to a 'recording agreement' with Rough Trade Records, Cabaret Voltaire released their first record, the single *Extended Play*; 'Headkick' referred to the death of Mussolini at the hands of Italian partisans, amongst whom were some of his former supporters, while other track titles such as 'Talkover' and 'The Set Up' gave a further indication of their ideas and attitudes. Their second LP, *Voice of America*, has been acclaimed as a landmark for its use of cut-up and voice-overs, first prescribed in the 1960s by William Burroughs in his book *Electronic Revolution*.

One of the main intentions of Cabaret Voltaire was to 'upset people in any way possible. To infuriate them, and to stimulate people. It was such a low period and we just felt forced to actually go and provoke people as much as possible.' (Chris Watson)[1]

During the last few years of the Seventies, Cabaret Voltaire

145. Cabaret Voltaire, press advert, 1980
146/147. Labels for *3 Crépuscule Tracks*, Les Disques du Crépuscule, 1981
'I had not designed the sleeve artwork for Cabaret Voltaire's second LP, *Voice of America*, which was a collage done by the group, but this image is an obvious extension of its songs like "Kneel to the Boss" and the public address system voice-overs on "This Is Entertainment". The labels for "Sluggin' fer Jesus" on the Crépuscule record were also an expression of man's struggle to be himself. These were designed through a combination of photocopying, drawing, and PMT overlays — breaking down the "quality" of the picture until only its basic outline remains.'

broke new ground in experimental music and film, thus encouraging countless imitators. They cited their third LP *Red Mecca*, as a tribute to Orson Welles' film *Touch of Evil*, but this was no plagiarism. The group's early videos were also widely praised — examples of which are held in the permanent collection of the Museum of Modern Art in New York.

'I think in people's senses there is a hierarchy, and the visual side is a lot more spontaneous — people react a lot more immediately to a visual image than to an audio image . . . I'm not saying it's longer lasting. There's a lot more crossover if you see and hear something together — it seems to be a more complete experience.' (Stephen Mallinder)[2]

There was a downside to this success — its powerful combinations were soon pastiched by more commercial purveyors of pop video, a then still emergent form. Dissatisfied with their cult status on the Rough Trade label, Kirk and Mallinder chose to meet the major's music business halfway by signing to Some Bizarre Records, which acted as an agency between the group and its promotion and distribution by Virgin Records. Watson, meanwhile, went on to work with Tyne-Tees Television as a sound engineer before linking up with Andrew McKenzie and Dr Edward Moolenbeek to reactivate the sound research group, The Hafler Trio, concentrating upon the use of sound as essential 'energy' rather than as a form of entertainment.

Cabaret Voltaire now record for EMI Records, who, in 1987, released the group's first LP under this new arrangement, *Code*.

Neville Brody, who has been responsible for the group's design since 1979, takes up the story:

'I had been very impressed with Cabaret Voltaire's music, and felt my work to be in sympathy with what the group were doing. However, I considered the sleeve designs of their records weren't doing them justice. Their style was too close to the current genre, which was largely indebted to their work anyway. The problem at the time was that fewer and fewer bands were staying true to the ideals they had set out with: amongst those that did were Throbbing Gristle, Z'ev, Boyd Rice, The Pop Group, Pere Ubu, and Cabaret Voltaire, but for most other groups, exploiting commercial possibilities had become a more important consideration. At that time, Fetish Records was just starting.

'I first rang up Rough Trade and then contacted the group directly and met up with them. They liked my work, and the first job I did for them was to design two posters. Rough Trade baulked at them — they said "too commercial", and thought the group were "selling out" just like the rest. Compared to other designs for Rough Trade's groups, mine were slick, but that was largely because the label had an anti-design policy and didn't want to be seen to give too much credence to packaging. Their overall quality control has always been a problem, in my opinion, but in the case of Cabaret Voltaire, I always dealt directly with the group.

'On every cover I have done for Cabaret Voltaire, the dominant theme is decay through process, the loss of human identity that results from communication being transmitted through machines that condition, not serve, human interaction. Decay through process is also about repetition, and the loss of quality that you suffer when information is abstracted from its human origin. Many of the ideas that were paramount in my work for Fetish also

applied to Cabaret Voltaire, forming a group identity in the way that a label identity is expressed.

'I didn't instigate all of their basic imagery. I acted more as a translator, which is often the designer's role, trying to achieve the best transition from a visual idea to its focus on the cover — and alongside ideas of decay through process, this was a contradiction I liked. The group, or usually Richard Kirk, would come up with an image that was passed on for me to work with. It was always close to my way of thinking, wanting to create another dimension for the music by using an abstracted form that worked laterally rather than literally. What I think distinguished Cabaret Voltaire's sleeves from many others at the time is that they avoided pomposity. We were trying to work against the kind of contrived and grandiose imagery that was signified on Ultravox sleeves, for example, seeking to engage an intuitive reaction that followed on from our own feelings about a sleeve's imagery. I had, and still have, a firm belief in the random factor as a way of subverting control — and the way repeating patterns tend to homogenise perception to the lowest common denominator. You have to break that dependence.

'As for the "independence" that was identified with Punk, it became too much of a buzzword used by the media that Punk was speaking out against. Punk was about individual expression, and more than anything, it was a reaction against authority. It couldn't really describe itself as "independent" unless the authority was completely circumvented — which, for a very short time, it was. But as soon as the whole phenomenon was categorised as "the independent scene", this ensured that it would become exactly the opposite. If the result you're working towards is widespread individual expression, you end up with anarchy, which for most people is a terrifying prospect. As the old adage has it, "freedom is frightening". This is why the "New Romantics" followed after Punk — as a way of counteracting that fear.

'So, with Cabaret Voltaire's covers, I was trying to involve this contradiction as well, mixing disturbing imagery with a use of colour and typography that was more of an exercise in marketing than Fetish ever was — partly because of the possibilities that full colour offered, and partly because of the advertising that followed on from a record's release. I was wanting to suggest the distinction between fact and belief.

'As far as Cabaret Voltaire's actual name was concerned, if anything, I found the association with Dada to be counter-productive to what I wanted to do with the sleeves. The Cabaret Voltaire was originally a club set up by Hugo Ball and others in Zurich in 1916. Obviously there were parallels, especially with regard to the group's live performances, but this Dada element was suggested anyway by the group's very choice of the name. They were not looking back. Earlier, Dada had also taught me a lot, especially about different perspectives and the ways in which you could express ideas, so it would have been pointless for me to return to first base. So as far as doing the group's artwork was concerned, they might just as well have been called "The Screaming Abdabs".'

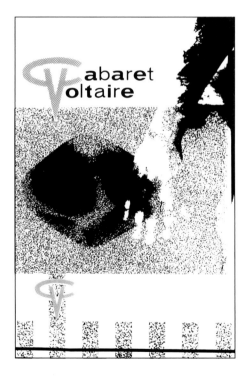

1 Quoted in Charles Neal, *Tape Delay* (SAF Publishers, 1987).
2 Quoted in *Industrial Culture Handbook* (Re-Search Publications, 1982).

148/149. *Opposite:* **Poster and badges, 1980**

'Only the human hand extends into the picture: it seems as if it is being doused in radioactive particles, clasping for a diamond.

Not many bands were using logos at this time — on the one hand, this alludes to the corporate image an organisation with a name like "World Media Enterprises" might have, but after I had designed it, somebody said that it was reminiscent of a drawing pin (thumbtack), and since then I haven't been able to see it any other way. Many people wore badges as an article of faith in the late 1970s and early 1980s — now it's gone right out of fashion. This, too, is related to the demise of picture sleeves.'

150. Poster for Cabaret Voltaire, 1980

'This is the closest I ever got to a direct illustration for the group, though the image didn't involve any specific point. It could be about biological warfare, it could be about technological destruction, and the sense of "where do you run?" — like Cary Grant fleeing from the crop-spraying airplane in Hitchcock's *North By Northwest*. This is always the trouble when you are trying to work intuitively — what *is* there to explain about work that involves an emotional response?'

151/152. *3 Crépuscule Tracks*, **Les Disques du Crépuscule, 1981**
'It was important to convey the fact that this was a 3-track EP, a separate item to the domestic Rough Trade releases. I was experimenting with the montage of different images that would inter-react, so on the front I used a photograph taken at an industrial fair, with two children looking at an exhibition of modern scientific developments. On the back cover, a man standing trial was combined with an aerial photograph of cultivated fields.'

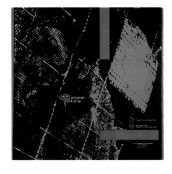

153. 'Red Mecca', Rough Trade Records, 1981
'Richard Kirk supplied me with a set of video-generated images which I had to decide how to crop and use. The cover shows two different treatments. I wanted to create a waterfall effect in colour, but very consciously in a video style with a garish and artificial quality to it that could be compared to a painterly use of colour. The type was simply stating "here is a piece of information". This was a double front cover, with a bled spine at the base rather than the side.'

154/155. *Jazz The Glass*, press adverts, 1981
'The adverts were combined from overlaying some photos I had found. This was for a single with two new songs, released after the LP as a 7″ in a lurid pink bag. At the same time, a 12″ was released in a clear plastic sleeve.'

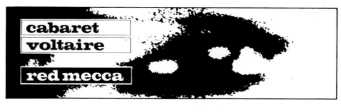

156. Sticker for 'Red Mecca', 1981

157. Label for 'Red Mecca', 1981

63

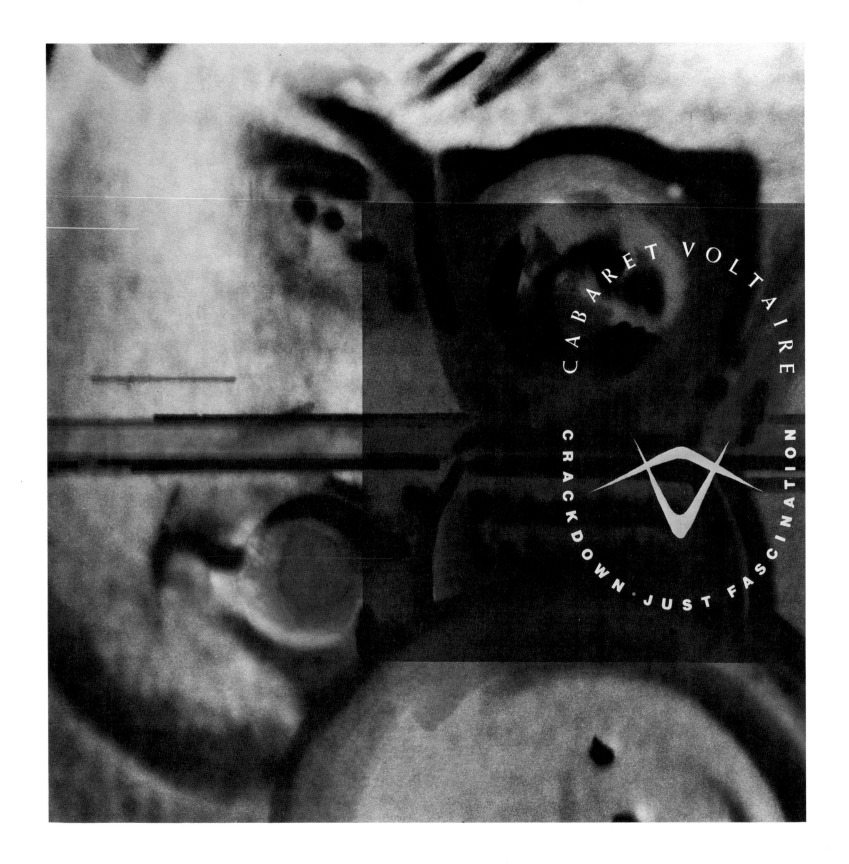

158. 12″ front cover for *Crackdown/Just Fascination*, Some Bizarre/Virgin Records, 1983
159. 7″ front cover for 'Just Fascination', Some Bizarre/Virgin Records, 1983
160. 12″ back cover for *Crackdown/Just Fascination*, Some Bizarre/Virgin Records, 1983

'I used small sections of the original images that the band had passed on to me, Stephen Mallinder's head for the front, and Richard Kirk's for the back cover. I cropped and enlarged the front image to the point where it became abstract and textural. The symbols were used to question the language of symbols more than anything else—to represent signification, also suggested by my designs for *The Face* at that time. The symbol on the front was developed from the letters C and V and "Just Fascination" was illustrating the focussing upon a point, where the direction extended outwards as well as inward. The type was used to give a sense of movement, and to form an arena around the symbols, but it's subservient to the rest of the cover. With record cover design, you would normally enlarge the 7" sleeve's artwork to the size of a 12". What we did was to enlarge the image whilst keeping the 7" artwork the same size on the 12".'

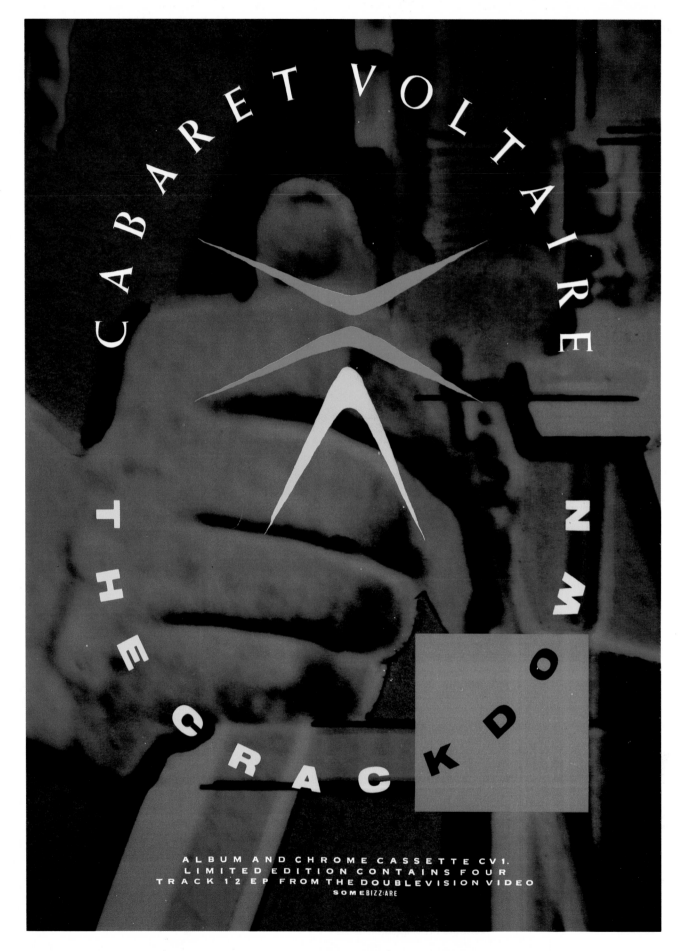

161. Poster for 'The Crackdown', 1983
'This design used another section of the image from the LP's inner sleeve. The romanesque serif type has a very deliberate cut. If you take the square away and imagine what is left, the design becomes very centred with an almost fascistic sense of perfection. The square questions this, undermining the precision of the poster's design. I was trying to challenge myself as much as anyone else.'

162/163. Cover and inner sleeve for *The Covenant, The Sword and the Arm of the Lord*, Some Bizarre/Virgin Records, 1985
'The video-generated images implied assassination and surveillance. The title of the LP refers, I think, to survivalists and revivalist preachers of the US Mid-West who mix their religious beliefs with a belief in Armageddon and a support for organisations like the CIA. Again, there is an imposed order to perception, and to the sleeve.'

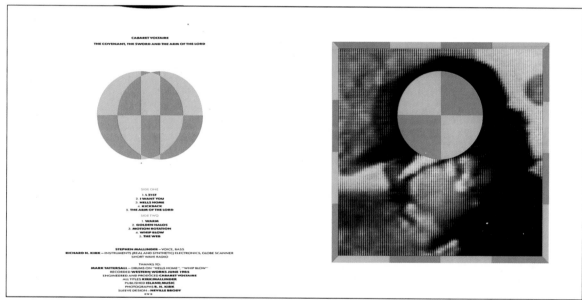

164. Inner sleeve for 'The Crackdown'
'This was formed out of two colour photographs which were not cropped on the fold, so that they didn't match as expected. Solid red was overprinted on the whole area. I drew up the looping type using Letraset at a very large size.'

'Speed is violence. The most obvious example is my fist. I have never weighed my fist, but it's about four hundred grams. I can make this fist into the slightest caress. But if I project it at great speed, I can give you a bloody nose. You can easily see that it's the distribution of mass in space that makes the difference. Every technology produces, provokes, programs a specific accident. The invention of the airplane was the invention of the plane crash.'
(Virilio/Lotringer, *Pure War*, Semiotext(e), 1983).

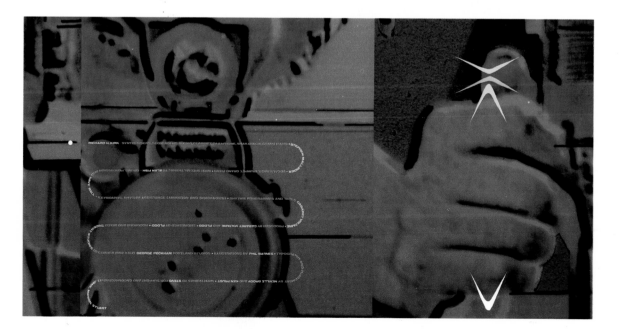

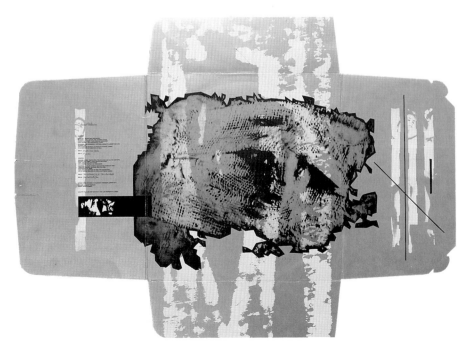

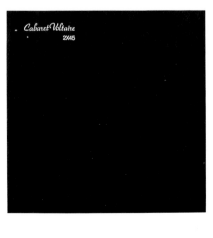

165/166. *2×45*, Rough Trade Records, 1986
167/168. Opened-out inner and front cover for *2×45*, Rough Trade Records, 1982
169. Labels for *2×45*, 1982

'The original sleeve for *2×45* was a fold-out in silver and black, with two 45 rpm records enclosed. Each had its own label in a pastel colour. By issuing a plain black outer front cover, I wanted to create a booby trap inside that followed no record cover conventions. Rough Trade liked it because it made for some very successful in-store displays and acted as a self-poster. The type on the outside was deliberately neutral with minimal information, contrasted with images on the inside that were originally three-dimensional, constructed in clay and wrapped in bandages. It wasn't crucial that they should be *immediately* recognisable as faces.'

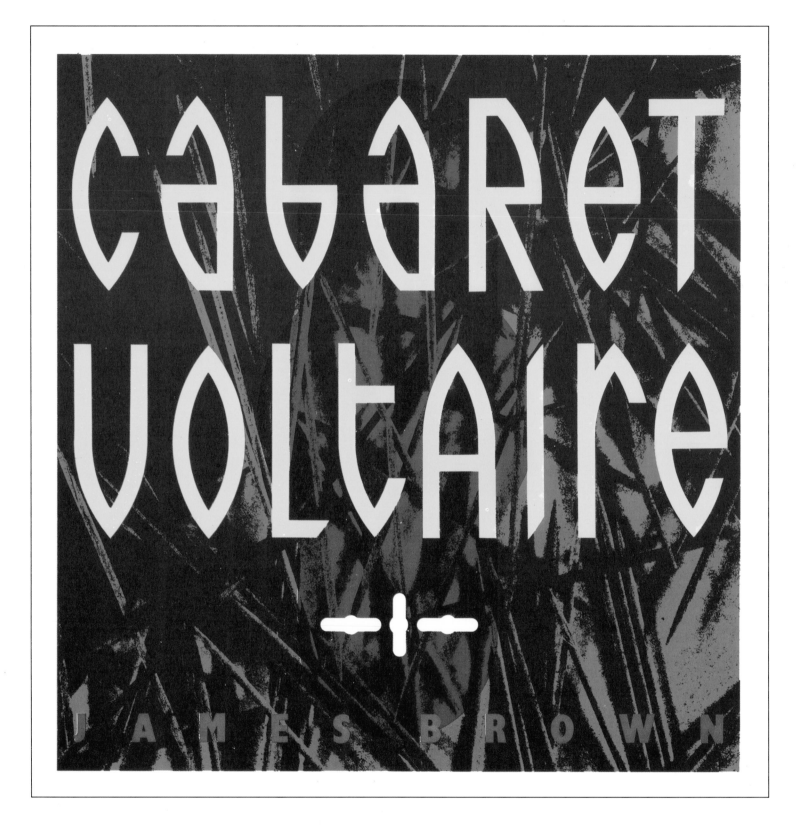

170/171. **12″ cover for** *James Brown*, **Some**
Bizarre/Virgin Records, 1984
172. **7″ cover for** *James Brown*, **Some Bizarre/**
Virgin Records, 1984
'I ignored the record's title for the same reasons
that I ignored the Dada reference. There's
something insidious about the cover, with the
shapes treated as if they were promoting a large
pharmaceutical or chemicals corporation. I wanted
the sleeve to suggest prickly heat — the interplay of
colours and shapes is apparently soft but actually
disturbing. The only element that connected it to
the LP that the song was taken from (fig.172) is the
type; by giving the border a frame the sleeve is
"contained", but also mock-precious.'

173/174. Cover and inner sleeve for
***Microphonies*, Some Bizarre/Virgin**
Records, 1984
'It looks as though there's a plug in the man's
mouth, but I don't think he's actually
dribbling. The targeting implies co-ordinates
seen on film footage relayed from outer
space. With the choice of colours, I wanted to
undermine danger in the same way that big
conglomerates package their products with
soothing colours. Where do the drugs stop?'

175/176. Symbol and front cover for *Code*,
EMI Records, 1987
The photograph was by Marc Lebon, and the
symbol designed with Cornel Windlin. This
was used prominently on the inner sleeve,
and broke up to form the word 'code'.

GENERAL

Most people's sense of musical history starts at the point when records became packaged in picture covers. This convention really started in the 1950s, when the introduction of 33 rpm LPs, and later, of stereo sound, boosted the popularity of records and created markets for more varied musical tastes. From the look of the sleeve, you had to be able to recognise whether the record was Country and Western, Jazz, or Rock 'n' Roll. The image, however, was still secondary to the music, which would usually be carefully annotated by sleeve notes on the back cover.

'The first sleeve that really captured my imagination was David Bowie's *Ziggy Stardust* in 1973. You could listen to the music on one level, but with the cover, the lyrics and the live show, everything inter-related so as to form a complete package. The first group I remember doing this were The Beatles with *Sgt. Pepper*. They had commissioned artists to do covers for them before this (notably Klaus Voorman for *Revolver*); however, their record company (EMI) strongly resisted the idea of using Peter Blake's cardboard cut-outs for *Sgt. Pepper*, fearing lawsuits from those stars who had been cut-out and caricatured for the cover photograph.'

It is ironic that this sleeve is now seen as the point where the music industry was finally able to celebrate its understanding of how to market a record successfully. Around the same time, record producers finally became central to a pop musician's fortunes, following on from George Martin and Phil Spector's initiatives. This further consolidated the marriage of sound to projected image.

'If you look back at traditional Sixties pop music covers, the general pattern was a photo of the band with a bit of type. If you look at a sleeve of the mid-Eighties, it's the same thing. We have come full circle, from expressing in visual terms ideas associated with the music, to conveying ideas that were as important as the music in the late Seventies and early Eighties, but at no time actually losing the human image on the cover. Now there are no ideas. Just the human image, conveyed by the personality of the performer.

'For a few years around the time of punk, the situation did improve immensely. You could go in with a new act and the A and R guy would listen to it and really take an interest — you got a fair hearing. Now it's worse than it was before punk. It's very very bad. You now ring up an A and R guy, and these are even A and R guys that I know and have taken acts to over the years, and they're too busy, or they're at lunch, or they can never be bothered to see the act. The only things that end up getting signed are people that are signed through favours. The bad old days are back where most of the record-company guys, with notable exceptions, are more interested in getting drunk and stoned and getting home early. One A and R guy that I know has a yearly pay packet of supposedly £120,000. To me that sort of figure is incalculable. And this guy probably spends a good part of his time with a biro tube up his nose.'

(Alan Edwards, 1984, quoted by Simon Garfield, *Expensive Habits, The Dark Side of the Music Industry*, Faber and Faber, 1986).

177. *Opposite:* **Zuice, 'Everyone a Winner',
Phonogram Records, 1986**
**178. Zuice, 'I'm Burning', Phonogram
Records, 1987**
**179. Zuice, 'Bless Your Lucky Stars',
Phonogram Records, 1987**
'I wanted to project an image with Zuice that
broke with the usual presentation of a British
soul band. The typography was as crucial as
the photograph of the group. On "I'm Burning"
(which was finally used as the sleeve for "I'm
a Survivor") the group photograph could be a
still from a movie. This was helped by working
with the choreographer Fwa Richards.'

**180/181. Defunkt, 'The Razor's Edge',
Hannibal Records, 1982**
'I based the painting on a photograph of
Defunkt's front-man, Joe Bowie. 'The Razor's
Edge' might have referred to cocaine rituals.
The record and its design were about the line
between the bright side and the darker side
of modern existence.'

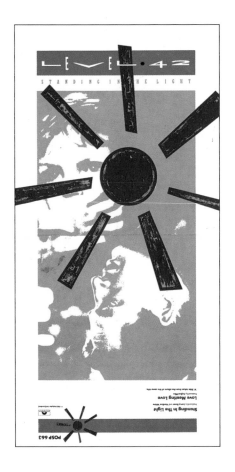

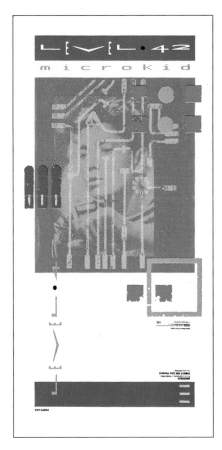

182. Level 42, 'Standing in the Light', Polydor Records, 1983
183. Level 42, 'Microkid', Polydor Records, 1983
'With both covers, I abstracted what I considered to be the main ideas behind the song. The Level 42 logo was designed as a unit in itself, with its own internal rhythm: the shape was more prominent than its readability.'

184. *Elephant Talk*, white label, 1983
The cover was the outcome of lengthy experimentation using the PMT camera.

185. Depeche Mode, *Just Can't Get Enough*, Mute Records, 1982
'The song and its sleeve were at odds with each other. The modular images portray exploitation and social bondage.'

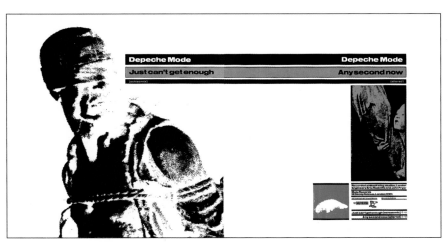

'From 1976 onwards, spanning the time when I started to design sleeves (which I think in many ways were a lot more important than the ones I'm doing now), you would never consider putting a photo of the band on the cover: record companies used to have to re-pack picture-sleeved covers into plain paper bags to give to Top of the Pops producers, who associated such sleeves with the kind of music they abhorred. A parallel period was the Sixties — take, for example, the underground records of that time, and even the more successful ones like *Strange Days* by The Doors — similar ideas were being nurtured. The language of rebellion is timeless, even if its stylistic conventions differ.

'Style evolves from content, or is dictated by content. Nowadays, the opposite is true, and never be persuaded that the style is the content. From 1976 to 1982, say, record covers would influence the way people think. Today, they influence the way people dress. To put it another way, previously we were talking about an inner self, and now it's all about the way the self is colonised. If you want to pursue ideas for ideas' sake rather than commercial gain, the audience is going to be small, unless you are already fully established or in a position to make a comeback. Reform, re-release old records, or do a cover version of an old song is the order of the day. To reach a large audience, you have to mimic the language of advertising — this has become accepted tradition of the day, and few are prepared to challenge it. Familiarity is the key. Record companies think "We have to reach a larger audience, and the way to do it is to put a picture of the band on the cover, because everyone who's wanted to reach a larger audience in the past has done this". And if you don't put the band on the cover, there is always the video to carry the personality.

'I remember one of my college tutors looking down on record cover design because he thought the music business was a nursery school industry. That might have been true twenty years ago, but in spite of its present power "the music biz" is still a short-cut for graphic designers; there is no strong system of indenture. I was very lucky in this respect — we were able to grow up and learn in public and benefited from the strong support of the

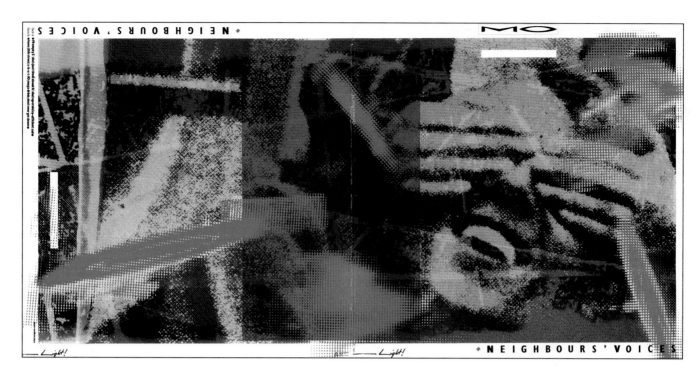

**186. David Mo, *Neighbours' Voices*, Light/
RCA France, 1984**
'The process that went into making this
image was an enjoyable one — unfortunately,
the typography turned out to be a poor
second cousin, and doesn't relate well to the
main theme — social pressure and the
onslaught of information.'

**187. Minimal Compact, *Next One Is Real*,
Crammed Discs, 1984**
'The sleeve is about social decay, and the
ritualistic elements that both celebrate this
and become impaired because of it. The
images were PMT exposures of clay-reliefs
that I had carved, the front being originally
the size of a brick.'

'There is no progress. the world changes
materially. Science makes advances in
technology and understanding. But the world
of humanity doesn't change. Morally, the
world is both better and worse than it was. We
are worse off than in the Middle Ages, or the
17th and 18th centuries, in that we have the
atomic menace. It is ridiculous that time an
time again we need a radioactive cloud
coming out of a nuclear power station to
remind us that atomic energy is
extraordinarily dangerous. So this shows the
imbecility, the stupidity of mankind. Why
should a civilisation that misuses its power
have, or deserve, a normal music?'.
(Pierre Schaeffer, interviewed by Tim
Hodgkinson, *Re Records Quarterly*, March
1987).

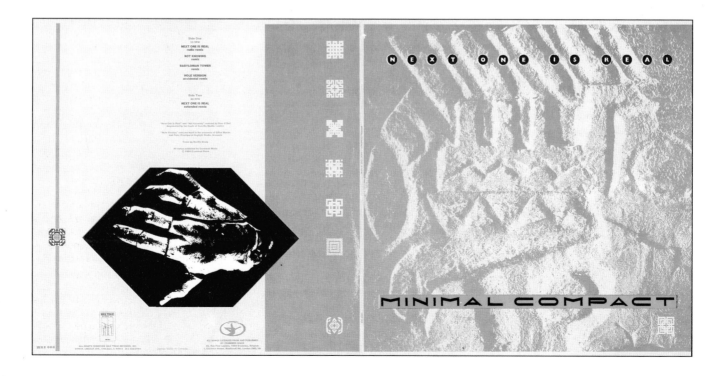

188/189. 7″ house-bag, Oval Records, 1984

190. African Connection, 'Dancing on the Sidewalk, Oval Records, 1984

191. *This is Soca! 84*, Oval Records, 1984

192. Kantata, *Asiko/Duke*, Oval Records, 1984

'Oval was a small independent label run by Charlie Gillett who is also a DJ on Capital Radio in London. It chose to deal with musical areas usually ignored by the major labels, releasing music from disparate sources, like Soca. They approached me, wanting to bring some unity to the label's identity, and with budget constraints similar to the ones I'd worked with at Fetish: it was nearly all two-colour. They decided they wanted to use house-bags, and I think this is some of the best work I did around this time. I cut out masking tape, went over it with a piece of black negative and scalpel, and then enlarged it. I wanted it to look bold and professional, but very tribalistic.'

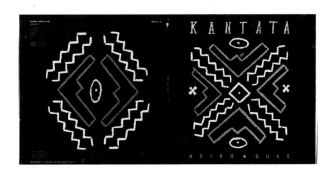

193/194. George Darko, 'Highlife Time',
packaged in 12″ house-bag, Oval
Records, 1984

**195/196. Marilyn, 'Baby U Left Me',
Phonogram Records, 1984
197. 7th Heaven, 'Hot Fun', Phonogram
Records, 1984
198. *This is Soca! 2*, London Records, 1985**

**199. Raybeats, 'Holiday Inn Spain', Don't
Fall Off the Mountain Records, 1981**
'I was using a felt pen on CS10 and scraping
away the ink with a blade. the looseness of
the painted brush strokes was then
manipulated into something that was
constantly moving. The mixed typefaces of
the titles predates their use in *The Face*.'

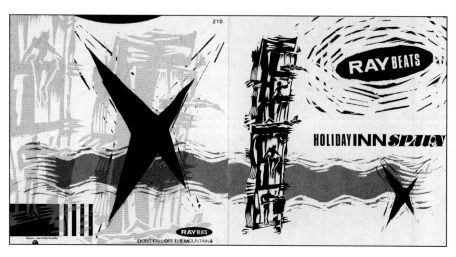

ideas at the time, and the record companies working them through. Now everyone's at it, and people tend not to notice the mistakes when 99% fall into that category. The whole business is as much about design, stylists, photographers, make-up artists, especially PR people, and now plastic surgeons – all are services to the presentation. The music is immaterial, purely packaging. The financial limitations imposed on Punk covers made you look for different approaches. When people do this now, they look to what best sells sex – usually soul music (rather than hip-hop), which is packaged the way perfume is advertised. All this money that's poured into the presentation is Protection, which is then afforded to the position of the business' chosen ones in the (un-)critical media – the praise lavished over Prince is a good example of this, and recently – too late in the day – those critiques for and against Bruce Springsteen have often done nothing more than consolidate his position, and thereby the USA's, at the top of the agenda. One step beyond Hype.

'Record cover design has always been about the communication of promise, but the real tragedy is that most people have now lost faith in the actual music and no longer look to it, or the cover, for ideas. Because Prince does record some great pop songs amongst all his self-indulgence, critics throw up their arms and say everything is great – confirmation of their own status. People have lost faith because there's little else but commercialism; however, in spite of the untouchability of cover stars, the same people that this exploits treat it all as fantasy. It's a fear of silence, not a fear of music.

'You have only to consider the huge influence record covers of the late Seventies have had on international design – the noise of styles that say absolutely nothing, except "PAY". When I first saw Malcolm Garrett and Linder's sleeve for *Orgasm Addict* by The Buzzcocks, I was still at college and my eyes popped out of my head. The way they were handling what I thought was sacred record company information, turning it sideways and vertical, was a confirmation for me that anything was possible.

'The only convention still left to be broken is the vinyl itself, and that will be phased out before long anyway; it's odd that compact discs are packaged in what are called "library cases", for there's a difference between silence and the speechless. However, when breaking down any conventions, you have to accept the possibility that not every rule is going to be better for having been broken. When you are diverted from carrying through new ideas, and the mainstream absorbs ideas that it fails to understand and which you have not yet fully developed, obviously the effect will be more confusion and a state of limbo where nothing grows. You are left with a new age of Mannerism – there are only gestures, and everyone is wondering when something is "going to happen". Of course, things are happening all the time, but people are taught that they are powerless. History has proved time and time again that they are not.'

200. Proposed cover for Parliament, *The Bomb*, Phonogram Records, 1985

23 SKIDOO

201. 23 Skidoo, 'The Gospel Comes to New Guinea', Fetish Records, 1981
'The title refers to the kind of innocence that is destroyed by colonialism, but I chose not to depict its usual Imperial connotations. These are, in a sense, colonial sleeves. This extends the double identities of the 'Zebra Club' sleeve (fig. 137) for The Bongos; I tried out various techniques of triple-layering on the PMT machine and spent a lot of time experimenting with different exposures and use of developing fluid. The result is double-edged – the hand is affirmative, but it might also be negative. You are never offered the choice.'

THE GOSPEL COMES TO NEW GUINEA

At various times, Tom Heslop, Alex and Johnny Turnbull, Fritz Haaman, Sam Landell-Mills, David Tibet and Sketch have worked together in different permutations as 23 Skidoo. Before recording for Fetish and then Illuminated Records, the group released its first single, 'Another Pretty Face', in 1981. 23 Skidoo's sound was volatile and varied, reflecting the group's changing line-up; at times, it had much in common with the angular funk of the Manchester band A Certain Ratio, at others it would veer more towards wall-of-noise group Last Few Days, their sometime associates, or rhythms ingested from African drummers or Indonesian gamelan. One year the group's concerts would be dance parties, the next, they would mix percussion and Tibetan thigh-bone with unsettling tape-loops – a period recorded on their 1983 LP, *The Culling is Coming*.

Other releases, *Seven Songs* and 'Coup' in particular, made a considerable impact, though the group always overlooked the temptation to become commercially minded because of this success. At one time 23 Skidoo were set to be pop stars, and in the next breath its members had all but vanished — whether to other groups, film projects or martial arts classes; for them, playing music was not a career.

Having affinities with similar sound combinations coming from New York in the early Eighties – those of the Contortions, the Bush Tetras and Liquid Liquid, for example – 23 Skidoo's mixing predates the larcenous language of hip-hop. In 1987, the group signed to Rush Management, the organisation behind the Def Jam record label.

'My overriding concern with 23 Skidoo was, from the outset, to extend the two-dimensional plane of record covers far more than I did on any other work for the Fetish label. The other groups' covers were using two-dimensional forms to create depth in two-dimensional space. I moulded the artwork for the early 23 Skidoo covers as three-dimensional objects and then photographed the results in different ways, hoping to transport the viewer further by extending a cover's possibilities beyond the usual limitations. I wanted to experiment by using the printing process to reproduce images derived from a three-dimensional source; I became quite obsessive about the ritualistic possibilities of this, especially when combined with the markings that were on the sculptures.

'I would then look for a found image that would precisely complement the emotional state I wanted to convey. As with Cabaret Voltaire's covers, the taking of the found image out of its initial context to inter-react with another element or process was carefully controlled. The found image might be from a Soviet magazine, a picture postcard, from television or from a newspaper, but it was the composition of its basic emotive elements that made for its choice.'

'The 23 Skidoo logo was important to this process. It defied the contemporary practice, where designers would use "proper" traditional typefaces, born of the need to make the independent scene appear more professional than the majors. From one 23 Skidoo cover to the next, the logo would be abstracted to the point

**202. 23 Skidoo, 'Last Words', Fetish
Records, 1981**
'The raven flew, while a dog sat on its tail.'
(Folklore quoted by Sergei Eisenstein in *The
Film Sense*, Faber and Faber, 1943).

**203. Original woodcuts for 'The Gospel
Comes to New Guinea'/'Last Words', 1981**

where its letters were no longer regular forms, but a sequence of symbols that promoted an overall recognition. I adopted the opposite approach to that of most corporate logos, but achieved a similar effect — the more you looked at it, the more you simply recognised it. The logo made little sense as words, and was doing something very different in its method of communication.'

204. Poster for 'The Gospel Comes to New Guinea'/'Last Words', 1981
'We could only afford a black and white poster to promote 23 Skidoo's first 12", so I designed it in the shape of a diamond to give it a distinctive and unconventional quality in spite of this.'

203. *Opposite: The Last Gospel, **T-shirt, 1981***
'I contrasted some very industrial shapes with the ritualistic markings that I'd been abstracting in the 23 Skidoo logo. The T-shirt design is made up of two faces, one of which is upside down, but instead of taking human forms, I was working with different abstract patterns and highlighting sections where their inter-relationship had appeared as a human shape. I liked the way that this remained ambiguous, so people could form their own conclusions — the purpose was to promote thought, and I didn't want as much clarity in the result as I put to its formation. An image and the response to it needs a continual process of relocation if it is to remain seen; the importance of context.'

THE LAST GOSPEL

'People are always asking *how* certain results
are obtained, seldom *why*. The first query
stems from the wish to do likewise, a feeling
of necessity, a wish to emulate; the second
wishes to understand the motive that has
prompted the act – the desire behind it. If the
desire is strong enough, it will find a way. In
other words, inspiration, not information, is
the force behind all creative acts.'
(Man Ray, 'The Enigma of Things', quoted in
Man Ray: Photographs, Thames and
Hudson, 1982).

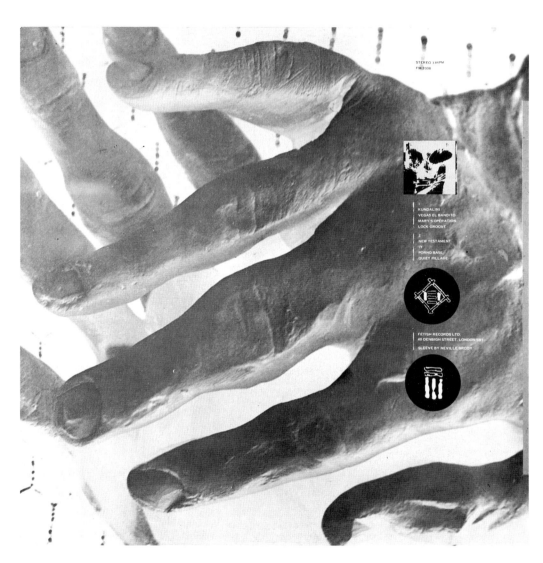

**206/207. 23 Skidoo, *Seven Songs*, Fetish
Records, 1982**
'This was a negative image of some clay hands that
I had made and then distorted, which can be seen
quite clearly in the thumb. The theme was
imprisonment and limitations, but also
celebration, which the drum symbol catalysed.
Seven Songs was a working title that was never
improved upon; I broke it down into seven
pictograms, which did not directly relate to the
record's individual tracks. I wanted people to work
out their own relationships. The boxing of the logo
follows on from the 12″ (figs. 201/202), where the
type doesn't fit the space designated for it. The
hand-drawn 'mini-LP' symbol worked totally against
the rest of the cover – Fetish were releasing lower-
priced LPs because we felt that most were vastly
over-priced.'

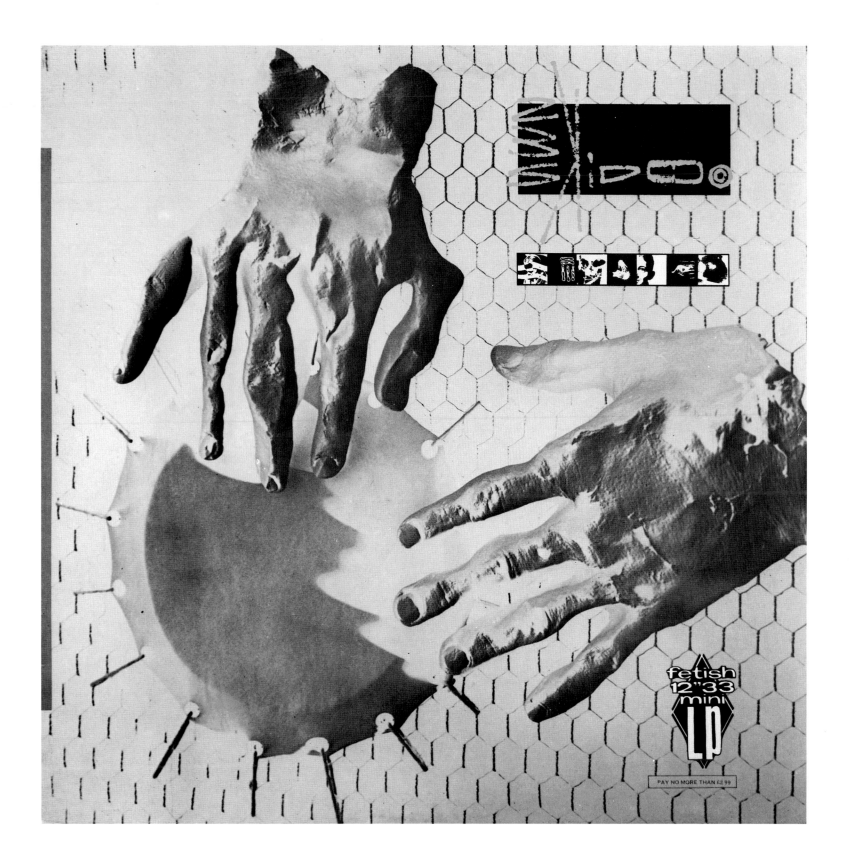

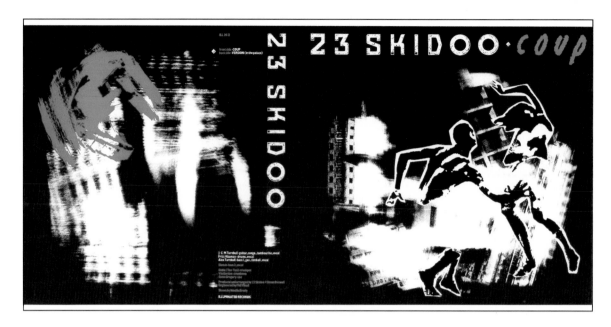

208. 23 Skidoo, 'Coup', Illuminated Records, 1984

'Having experimented further with the PMT machine, I took the buildings to violent decay. I had chosen post-Corbusier architecture as a reflection of the technological and sociological advances that I felt were going to implode: cold, mechanical buildings, lacking humanity. I directly contrasted that explosion of energy with the sexual connotations of dancing figures on a Latin-American record the group had shown me. The black-and-white of the sleeve, and its white border, make this even more acute. The hand-drawn type is reminiscent of the style of lettering used on war machinery – 1930s tanks.'

209. 23 Skidoo, *Urban Gamelan*, Illuminated Records, 1984

'A lot of people hate this cover; I liked the contrast of the front and back as total opposites of the same thing. Because of this, and the LP's title, the design seems to be more about style than anything else. At the time of the record's (much delayed) release, other groups like Einstürzende Neubauten from Berlin and Test Department from South London were using metal percussion with much more aggression, which forced unfair comparisons. 23 Skidoo were very involved with martial arts at this point, not only their combative side, but their means of releasing movement and concentrating discipline towards inner growth. *Urban Gamelan* was as much about a state of awareness as it was a musical phrase – 'gamelan' being the indigenous music of Java and Bali.'

23 SKIDOO

JUST LIKE EVERYBODY

210. 23 Skidoo, *Just Like Everybody*, B.C. Records, 1987
'This was a compilation of 23 Skidoo's best recordings. The cover had to be cost-conscious and commercially striking, so I tried to give it the feeling of a colourful "bootleg". The type is powerful and confident — like an American football player's shirt; its positive, physical force is made even stronger by the exploding sun. All the artwork was prepared on a photocopier.'

211/212. Label and front cover for 'Vs. The Assassins With Soul', Illuminated Records, 1986
'The star is usually a symbol of glamour, but in this instance it is a martial arts weapon. I wanted to create a challenge to the record's title, so that it might easily be thought of as 'Assassins *of* Soul'. The versus, 'VS', is the most pronounced type on the cover, and the 'Assassins' lettering an imitation of a Kung-Fu movie poster. The group's hand-drawn logo is further developed, and within the large bracket there is a pair of frightened and vulnerable eyes.'

BOOKS

From a design point of view, books are primarily about establishing a clear typographic system. Book design is of course a very different proposition to working on magazines, which have a different structure and a much stronger bias towards the use of images. Except in such cases as the Re-Search publications and similar music books where publishers have tried to marry the two media, photographs are sometimes used in books to provide "breathing spaces" within the text, whereas in magazines they generally carry a lot more editorial momentum.

'The design is largely a matter of pure common sense. The grid must be well proportioned on the page, with adequate inner and outer margins. You must find out in advance how the book is to be bound, so that you know whether its pages will open easily or whether you must exaggerate the margin away from the spine. Each book's character is largely developed out of detailing, such as the placing of headings and the choice of typeface. The jacket or cover is either the first or the last thing you do, and should signal the design and content as a whole.

'It is important to remember that as a designer you are working not only with a different temporal requirement, but, in most cases, a more deliberate and personal kind of expression. With this is mind, the design has to strike the right balance between passivity and intrusion. In the case of magazines that are around for a limited period, the design of an article or feature must immediately encourage the reader to read it — you can never take it for granted that this will happen. With books, you can, or at least you should be able to. Book design must support the act of reading its printed pages, which naturally demands more time than it takes to get through a double-page spread in a magazine.

'Space is as important a factor in a book as it is anywhere else. The design must be finely weighted so that the type has an impressive overall appearance, but not so much that it encourages the reader to stare at the page at the expense of the words themselves. If you are going to choose a typeface other than a sympathetic book fount like Garamond, Times or Bodoni Book, then you must be sure that the content supports such a deviation. The subject matter might be so indistinct that it helps to produce a more expressive element — a typeface such as Corvinus or Rockwell, for example. As usual, you work to the given task, not to the given norm.

'There is another side to book design which does not usually arise in magazine work — the choice of paper stock. The texture of the paper should support the book's literary style and the typeface(s) chosen for it. For example, it would be no use selecting Bodoni, with its very fine serifs, if you planned to print on a rough matt surface — unless, of course, you actually intended the type to break up. Once again, if you are going to opt for a more distinctive design, you have to consider the book's potential lifespan. With any design, a good question to ask yourself is "What will it look like in five years time?"

'I must say that I much prefer doing a cover to designing an entire book. Who wouldn't? Designing a 200-page book involves a great amount of work for what is usually a small return. Some publishers are their own worst enemies — although it is important to "never judge a book by its cover", the opposite most often applies now. The inside design is still somehow taken for granted, as if the writer had already designed the page. When the designer's function is encouraged as a profession, not unlike that of a doctor or a solicitor, it becomes a service industry that keeps it apart from the creative process.

'The future of the book as a means of communication is itself in the balance.[1] Perhaps it has already been lost to the more "democratic" emotions of popular music. More and more information, once the domain of books, is being transferred to computer disc and microfilm. You cannot browse through data banks.'

213/214. Catalogue for Stephen Buckley exhibition, *Many Angles*, the Museum of Modern Art, Oxford, 1985
The front cover had a cut-out shape that revealed the half-title page, shown below. It was printed on 300 gsm chipboard.

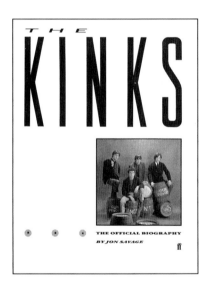

215. Cover for *The Kinks (The official biography)*, published by Faber and Faber, 1984
'*The Kinks* was a history of the group written by Jon Savage. Most of the photos were in black-and-white, with duotone reproductions used for many of the photographs in order to create a sense or re-presentation, as if something had altered over the years. There was quite a cluster of music books published around that time, so I wanted to give *The Kinks* a certain quality that combined pop with classicism. We used a lot of white space, but reversed type out of bars for the page numbers to 'hold' the text. The cover design itself seems a bit naive to me now — perhaps accidentally in keeping with the group's own history.' 'Where Have All The Good Times Gone?'.

---

1 See George Steiner's essay, 'After the Book?', written in 1972 and included in the anthology *On Difficulty* (Oxford University Press, 1978).

216. Cover for *A Report From The Bunker With William Burroughs* by Victor Bockris, Vermilion Books, 1982

A Report From The Bunker was crucial to other areas of Brody's work. The job was sub-contracted from Hipgnosis, a design company that became well known in the Seventies for its record covers for, amongst others, Pink Floyd and Peter Gabriel. Brody chose to take a 1950s detective-story cover style: it was quite a liberty to use this pulp-fiction idiom and apply it to a writer of the stature of William Burroughs. He wanted to suggest something seedy and in disrepair, unusual in the case of a book that is more or less a biography, the aim of which is generally to eulogise its subject.

216/218. Cover for *Mr Love and Justice* by Colin MacInnes, Penguin Books, 1986
(new edition; originally published in 1960).

217/219. Cover for *City of Spades* by Colin MacInnes, Penguin Books, 1986
(new edition; originally published in 1957).

'I followed through ideas similar to those I had chosen to use for the William Burroughs book. I wanted to create a 1950s atmosphere, re-interpreted for the 1980s. The books were relaunched to coincide with the film *Absolute Beginners*, and there was a lot of Fifties nostalgia in evidence at the time. To his eternal credit, there was no pressure from the art director at Penguin Books to give the cover the "Book of the Film" treatment, in spite of the strapline. To my surprise, he said that the "8 Eyed Spy" covers (see figs. 129/130/131) that I had designed for Fetish had encouraged him to commission me, and it was good to be able to rework those ideas with the luxury of full colour. However, I mainly used washes over a black-and-white base, so the colour became secondary to the light and tone, a resonant illustration to hark back to the Fifties paperback and B-movie — not as nostalgia for a bygone age, but to question the idea of categorising social currents into decades.'

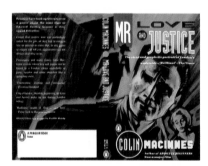

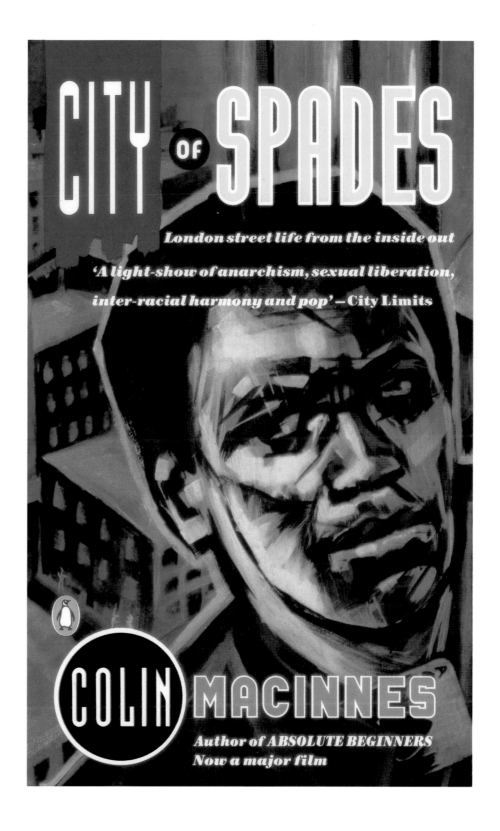

220. Cover for *Up-Tight* by Victor Bockris/ Gerard Malanga, Omnibus Press, 1983
Victor Bockris had been impressed by the cover Brody had designed for the William Burroughs book, and therefore asked him to work on this biography of The Velvet Underground, an American group that had become famous in the Sixties; indeed many Punk bands cited the group as 'a main influence', and in 1988, the group's legacy shows no signs of fading. Brody gave The Velvet Underground a hard black-and-white treatment that reflected their East Coast origins, using photographs like snapshots from The Factory, but hinting at the reverse effect to the one adopted for *The Kinks* book. In this case, the myth replaces memory, and promise becomes a coded possibility.

221. Poster for Henri Cartier-Bresson exhibition, the Museum of Modern Art, Oxford, 1984
223/224/225. Front cover and inside spreads for exhibition catalogue, the Museum of Modern Art, Oxford, 1984
'I used an apparently conventional typographic style, which was offset by an imposing area of white space. Page numbers were reversed out of black blocks, which are held to the outer corner of each page to maintain the structure.'

226. Proposed cover for Comedia Books, 1986
The book, by John A. Walker, was never published. Its theme was the connections between art and pop music, concentrating on the histories of groups and pop performers who had studied at art college — John Lennon, David Bowie, Roxy Music and the Sex Pistols, to name a few. The original plan had been to issue the book to coincide with the exhibition, held in London at the Camden Arts Centre in December 1986, entitled *Interaction*. Instead of simply printing a catalogue, the gallery took the unusual step of commissioning a sound recording by The Hafler Trio, *Brain Song*.

227. Cover for *Let's Join Hands* by John Fordham, Elm Tree Books/Hamish Hamilton, 1986

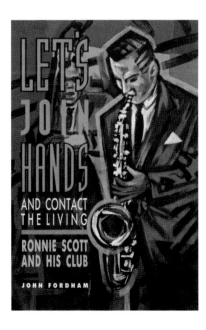

MAGAZINES

In the 1985 film, *Desperately Seeking Susan*, the actress Rosanna Arquette intercepts a 'lonely hearts' advert and is able to assume the more glamorous and emancipated identity of its subject, Madonna, by wearing the jacket that the latter had traded for a pair of cowboy boots. The invisibility of Arquette's past persona, obscured by this change of appearance, and the renewed self-confidence and determination that it brings, signifies the promise of transformation at the centre of fashion and its styles. More common, however, is the absence of any clear direction — typified by the confusion of past styles and eras evident in the modern city's High Street chain stores. The 1980s have the faceless image of an era in which most people would rather be somewhere else; confronted with the city's monotony of hourly news bulletins and traffic reports, everyone becomes an escapologist, reflected by the holiday features that appear regularly in most Sunday newspapers and in monthly magazines.

Style has become increasingly imperative. It is a movement away from 'who you are' towards 'what you might become' or 'what you could appear to be'; but this is no adventurous form of travel, rather a visual tourism that confirms the common desire to escape urban anonymity. Coupled with this is the media's ever-expanding pluralism; it promises the greater emancipation of 'specialist' fields of interest, but pluralism in effect becomes an ever-tightening spiral. Coverage is granted as if by decree — ideas, however, are usually neutered by their subjection to the lowest common denominator, easy entertainment. For those whose films/books/records attempt to directly address a situation and an audience's personal response to it, publicity becomes a form of deprivation. How many people will go to see a film only after reading a review of it? More choice seems to mean fewer surprises.

Magazines, which have always been bought to pass the time on the way to work or to support a lifestyle in the lounge at home, give expression to the desire for escapism. Their market is now enormous, with more titles appealing to a wider variety of 'target audiences' than ever before. Their renewed ascendancy over the past ten years, however, has been more than just a response to the demands of an avid readership. Unlike the brief advertising slots on television, the magazine medium provides something more lasting, something that is not thrown away the same day, or week, and costs less than a billboard. Magazines will even advertise themselves. More importantly, the sequential structure of a magazine is the kind that most closely resembles television's programming. A news story may be followed by a documentary, star profile or soap opera, and not only does each feature have a headline, there is a front cover as well. A world within.

Advertising is crucial to most products and publications in terms of financial feasibility, both before and after release. Most products, however, have increasingly become little more than self-advertisements — Levi's jeans are a prime example. The return to corporate sponsorship of the arts is another feature of advertising's power to control cultural expression; the plunder of a magazine's editorial and design personality is, however, closer to home.

The magazine format is similar to television's, for it also mirrors city life, always moving from one point to the next through different systems of information. City life needs an editor. The revival of the magazine industry reflects the way that everyday life has become abbreviated to a magazine format — a revival symptomatic of society's immersion in television language, but not its cause. Nevertheless, its impact has since passed the stage where it could be said to be simply 'giving the public what it wants'. This is the common excuse; as with tradition, what is

229/230. Spreads for the *Tatler*, November 1986

really meant is that it gives the public what it is *used to*. A new sensibility is necessary. The starting point might be found in one area of this market, where editors and designers have tried to carry through the momentum of ideas that the Punk movement made possible, applying them to the more exacting commercial and time-intensive demands of the mainstream visual media.

For many years, magazines depicted 'lifestyle' as a hobby separate from work. In the 1970s women's magazines and Sunday supplements refined a leisure-time formula that promised to provide more entertainment. Their history of practical information ('a few handy tips for our readers') moved away from the domestic labour-saving needs of the 'average' worker to satisfy the aspirations of a new life in the media, where everyone was made to seem a potential entrepreneur. In the mid-Seventies, office workers were encouraged to own a pressure cooker that would have the hot-pot ready upon returning home. In the mid-Eighties, they were told that to own a Filofax was paramount, a 'personal organiser' for the individual as Organisation: a world within. This controlled approach to life, and the magazines that advise readers what appointments are best met, are both a means of escaping the rigours of living in a no-longer glorious Britain, and a celebration of all the motives it holds most dear.

With the impact of Punk on pop culture, its liberating energy was assimilated into style and translated into the faked energy of chat shows. As far as the magazine world was concerned, Punk style afforded a host of new recipes just before Lifestyle became the staple fare. If constantly changing styles were, for some, a reaction against the stark imagery of original Punk, then for the media's executives, these styles allowed for the consolidation of an economy reliant on disposable trends. And it is not only products and magazines that become self-advertisements, but also individuals. Do you wannabe-like Madonna?

'We need not be detained too long in figuring out why [American television is loved]. In watching American television, one is reminded of George Bernard Shaw's remark on his first seeing the glittering neon signs of Broadway and 42nd Street at night. It must be beautiful, he said, if you cannot read.'
(Neil Postman, *Amusing Ourselves To Death*, Methuen, 1985).

'More media seems to mean worse media, as the same rations of jam are spread over an increasing mountain of processed white bread. The industrial base of pop music has been changing, as record companies – dragged screaming into the video age – have been forced to encounter, and work with, the film and television industries. Pop music, and the music industry, are no longer a separate entity, but part of a huge industrial conglomerate which spans the whole media. The age of pop being an unimportant sideline – where children can play in their own dirt – is over.'
(Jon Savage, 'Is There Life After Smash Hits?', *The Face*, No.62).

In 1977, the difference between a good and a bad review in the *New Musical Express* was for independent record companies (in particular) the difference between success and immobility. Today, music coverage is no longer exclusive to the music business and its press – a review in *Cosmopolitan*, or even better, a feature in *The Face*, is worth as much as if not more than a write-up in the *NME*. The growth of this phenomenon comes from two completely antithetical sources, combining to create a complex amalgam of cultural and subcultural forces. This brings with it a set of contradictions that makes any experimentation difficult. The propensity with which this has been attempted in *The Face* has to be borne in mind as one of its prime motivations – its passage from 'Rock's Final Frontier' to 'Best Dressed Magazine' (subtitles used at different stages of the magazine's history) ex-

emplifies the grounds upon which any future experimentation within the mainstream media might be attempted.

When the independent record sector began to struggle for survival after its successes in the late Seventies, new initiatives emerged in magazine publishing that have had a significant effect on popular culture. Neville Brody found himself in a unique position to break new ground, helped by the changing focus away from the newsprint music press to glossy magazines that qualitatively had more in common with Sunday supplements than with Punk's harbinger, the *New Musical Express*. Having joined *The Face* as designer, eighteen months after the magazine's successful launch in 1980, Brody converted his good fortune and went on to develop a design style that has become the decade's most influential. His design for *The Face* not only irrevocably changed the focus of magazine publishing from being always editorially-led, it made a greater use and created an increased awareness of visual language, leading inevitably to his becoming much in demand to design other publications eager to boost their sales. By then Brody's graphics, and most of all his typography, effected areas at such opposite commercial extremes as High Street shops and avant-garde art galleries. Such an outcome is the key to the contrasting approach *The Face* itself followed with its composition and coverage.

Alongside Punk's musical intervention in 1977 – in any case, the noise was secondary to the ideas behind it – came a surge of fanzines that were self-publishes and xerox printed. The *New Musical Express* – owned by IPC, which also publishes some of Britain's best-selling women's magazines – effectively assimilated the fanzines' areas of coverage. However, the fanzines' mix of provincialism (which never intended to compete with London's hated hegemony) and their cross-media coverage, which included politics, film and fashion alongside the music, had a marked influence. They presented a localised and highly personal view of the world that was exactly the opposite in terms of its reference points. With hindsight, their simple intention of direct action in the face of the alienating mainstream has had a circular effect. In spite of their success in the late Seventies, nothing has changed. Information has simply become more fragmented, and the fanzine boom has been just one small part of this chain of events.

As the newsprint music press went into decline, the glossy, visually-orientated and chart-based *Smash Hits* capitalised on the fading energy of Punk's ability to beat the majors at their own game, namely, image building. The fortnightly magazine appealed to a teenage audience that newsprint writers had largely abandoned in their quest for legendary status, and under the founding editorship of Nick Logan, *Smash Hits* developed its base to become Britain's biggest-selling pop magazine. Logan, seeking new challenges, would later show that his talent for recognising trends would have an even greater impact with *The Face*, which he set up with a minuscule budget of £7,000 in 1980. In tandem with Neville Brody's design, *The Face*'s reinvention of magazine language was to have an international influence that dictated a thousand stylistic variations. It did not simply update the existing Top Of The Pops idiom into a more energetic format, as *Smash Hits* had done. Its editorial style combined pop consumerism with a critique of its culture that most forcefully expressed the upheavals going on in everyday life – the after-effect of Punk, where the commercial had become even more plastic (Duran Duran). *The Face* both questioned this and celebrated the growing profusion of styles in the same breath – the worst effects of 'Style Culture' in the same issue that included items on 'radical footwear' and 'travelling hats', and this in *The Face*'s 80th number. Undermining and affirming people's assumptions of *The Face* throughout his five years with the magazine was Neville Brody's design.

THE FACE

Neville Brody's work for *The Face* questioned the traditional structure of magazine design.

'Everything in *The Face* was reasoned; every single mark on the page was either an emotive response or a logical extension of the ideas. If I was bleeding type off the edge of the page, it wasn't a case of "Oh, let's bleed type off the page". I was wanting to suggest three things. Firstly, how much of a headline do you need to be able to recognise it? Secondly, I wanted to give the idea that with each spread of *The Face* there was an infinite choice, and what we had done was to section out *one small part of that*; and lastly, I wanted to use the three-dimensional space of a magazine. Magazines are 3D items in space and time – there's a connection between page 5 and pages 56 and 57, a continuum. A magazine doesn't have to divide up space on a page like a newspaper, and the information it carries has more time to make connections between the different ideas that might be present. Why be inhibited by the edge of the page?

'There was a built-in order to what I was doing, and a relationship to all the elements, a balance and a rhythm. If Classicism represents the 'ideal' of a constant tradition and Romanticism a desire for change, I chose to work between the two. Within magazine bounds, I think *The Face* was very classical, because it still performed the basic functions that a magazine should work with. People missed that completely. To their credit, *New Sounds New Styles* and *iD*, two of *The Face*'s competitors, went much further in challenging the actual body text, rendering it unreadable in many places, but it was a main priority in *The Face* that you should read it. Editorial and design worked hand in hand – it was never a case of copy being handed over and that was that.

'The text itself wasn't presented emotively. What was surrounding the writing would affect and colour your appreciation, but if you isolated the writing itself, you should be able to judge it purely on what it was saying. *The Face* had two narratives, the writing and the design. We wanted people to be their own editors.'

'The grid was based on a simple system that could be adapted when necessary. The magazine started off with a four-column grid, was then firmly established as a three-column grid, and became a three and a two once the four-column had been abandoned completely. Exceptions were 'Intro' and the review-based 'Monitor' section, which needed the flexibility of allowing small pictures to be dropped in. The whole thing allowed you to centre design elements on the page very easily, and allowed for the inclusion of good medium-sized photographs.

'*The Face* had a very distinctive and quite unusual policy of allowing photographers a free hand – apart from briefing them beforehand, if necessary, rather than heavily adapting their work later. We felt that this would achieve a much better and more adventurous result. We did not want the photographs to become subservient to the identity of the magazine. We did not want to pursue the punk quality of photomontage, or to make the photographs graphic. The very act of giving photographers a free hand meant that they were already stepping out of the accepted norm. Montage was used in other ways. Design was working alongside the photography – again 'the third mind'. I felt that if I started to interfere with the photos, the design would be overstepping its mark when it didn't need to.

THE FACE No. 59

GERMANY 5.80 DM

● MARCH 1985 85p US $2.75

THE FACE

KILLER

SAM SHEPARD AND JESSICA LANGE
HOLLYWOOD'S HOT COUPLE

**Alison Moyet
Andy Warhol
Lovers rock
Pogues ◆ Brazil
Mel Smith**

HARD

Photo Jamie Morgan

233/234. 'Killer' cover, *The Face*, No.59, March 1985
This cover typifies the conviction of *The Face*'s tag-line, 'The World's Best Dressed Magazine'. It featured the new omnipresent Felix for the first time, and shows the strong influence that Buffalo had on the magazine — stylist Ray Petri with, in this case, photographer Jamie Morgan.

Hard is the graft when money is scarce. Hard are the looks from every corner. Hard is what you will turn out to be. Look out, here comes a buffalo! "The harder they come, the better" (Buffalo Bill)

'The photographs provided a base-line, along with other anchors that were used, like the text, or even the specific size and shape of the page. This laid the foundation for the experimentation I wanted to bring to other areas. I tried to treat the design of *The Face* very much like town-planning, guiding the reader around a particular issue. There needed to be directional symbols, and open space at a particular point — always at the beginning of a piece, where I would use white space to articulate an entrance: you don't put the doorway to a large building in a small alley-way. When you see magazines where every inch is filled, it shows that they are editorially led, or rather, editorially misled. In your own living room, you position things in the way you feel most comfortable, which enables you to appreciate and use the objects around you. With design, you establish a system, the system is your structure, you use it as your scaffolding, and then start building. You must still articulate the idea that a stairway leads up to the next floor, and you put your walls in once you have a relationship between the design elements that doesn't weaken the structure of the building.

'My reason for creating this apparently mathematical structure for the design wasn't only because people's perceptions feel more comfortable with a use of space that is weighted in this way. It would look strange, for example, to use heavy black symbols at the head of a text page that was set in a light serif typeface. A building needs to be seen to resist the effects of gravity, and people's appreciation of things is geared by what they already know. I needed a sound structure to enable experimentation on the next level.'

235. Kraftwerk, *The Face*, No.23, March 1982
Brody approached this on the basis of it being a poster. The spread shows a strong Constructivist graphic approach, shifting the alignment from editorial to the twin focus that the design was creating alongside it.

236. Julie Burchill column, *The Face*, No. 20, December 1981
This was the first time condensed and expanded type were used alongside each other.

237. Funkapolitan spread, *The Face*, No.16, August 1981
Brody's first spread included graphic forms of illustration to interact with other elements.

238. Kim Wilde spread, *The Face*, No.23, March 1982
'The period when Neville joined *The Face* was a tough one. On top of everything else, the design wasn't working well. I had got bored with the original look and was trying to make changes myself — not very successfully. Then, Neville left Stiff and was interested in doing some layouts on a freelance basis. He was learning his way and at this stage the spreads looked more like LP sleeves. His first cover, for Haircut One Hundred (see fig.242) which had the type on the left hand side, was fairly revolutionary.'
(Nick Logan, July 1987).

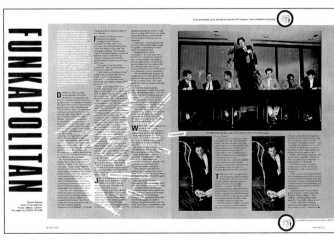

PROCLAIM	PRESENT	TIME	OVER
PROCLAIM	PRESENT	TIME	
OVER	PROCLAIM	PRESENT	
TIME	OVER	PROCLAIM	
PRESENT	TIME		

PROCLAIM	PRESENT	TIME	OVER
PROCLAIM	TIME	PRESENT	OVER
PROCLAIM	OVER	TIME	PRESENT
PROCLAIM	PRESENT	OVER	TIME
PROCLAIM	TIME	OVER	PRESENT
PROCLAIM	OVER	PRESENT	TIME

(Brion Gysin, extract from 'Present Time', *The Third Mind*, John Calder, 1978)

There is always a gap between intention and effect. Brody's main concern was to encourage *The Face*'s readership to look twice at a page. '*The Face* was often criticised for being difficult to read and to approach. This view is based on an advertising criterion, which has been around a lot longer than *The Face* has. We were never trying to sell our readers anything except the overall quality of the magazine. We were trying to make things as interesting as possible, and the reader had to look at every element that went into the magazine's composition. If it took somebody half-an-hour to understand a layout, or a second glance to read a headline, that was good, the reader had to work at it. People complained that the writing was style-obsessed, but there was always another side to it, both within the written content of the magazine and its design. You have to work at it, but we're not in the business of making life easy.'

The fact that Nick Logan never undertook any market-research for *The Face* supports this view. *The Face*, as Logan said on the Terry Wogan TV show, simply intended to be the "best magazine going". However, there are structural limitations to any magazine work that make *The Face*'s maintenance of variety and contrast a constant difficulty — and as Brody has suggested above, *The Face* did not readily settle for easy options.

'The features for each issue would be written within the month prior to publication. *The Face* deliberately had a very short production time. It needed to be as immediate as a weekly, with all the disadvantages of being a monthly. When the magazine started, it was like a local newspaper that wanted to appeal to the people that it wanted to write about, who would then go out and buy it. *The Face* then became witness to the death of street style as much as anything else. It was all part of the transition from low-budget culture to the multinational version of "Youth Culture". The so-called "style magazines" of the early Eighties, like *iD* and *The Face*, did not coin the phrase — it was foisted upon them.

'The magazine had a very small core of people working on it at the beginning. Later, this was translated from the consumer's viewpoint into being the biggest style manual of the time, and it became over-revered. People referred to it as "the style bible". They wanted an instruction book with a set of rules that could be changed every week.

239. 'African Chic', *The Face* No.24, April 1982
240. Contents page, *The Face*, No.24, April 1982
241. 'African Uprising' spread, *The Face*, No.25, May 1982

Brody was concentrating upon the use of one typeface — Grotesque — which he contrasted, above, with loosely hand-rendered Helvetica. This unpolished typography questioned the habit whereby everything in a magazine is typeset and slickly presented. The illustration for fig. 241 was by Ian Wright.

242. No.26,
June 1982,
Sheila Rock

243. No.29,
September 1982,
Sheila Rock

244. No.30,
October 1982,
Mike Laye

245. No.32,
December 1982,
Simon Fowler

 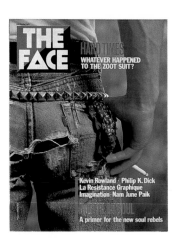  

246. No.33,
January 1983,
Peter Ashworth

247. No.34,
February 1983,
Derek Ridgers

248. No.36,
April 1983,
Jill Furmanovsky

249. No.40,
August 1983,
Davies/Starr

 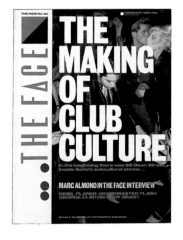  

250. No.41,
September 1983,
Steve Tynan

251. No.42,
October 1983,
Peter Ashworth

252. No.43,
November 1983,
Margit Marnul

253. No.44,
December 1983,
Steve Pyke

  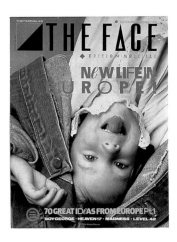 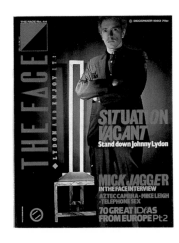

254. No.45,
January 1984,
Jamie Morgan

255. No.48,
April 1984,
Jamie Morgan

256. No.49,
May 1984,
Neville Brody

257. No.50,
June 1984,
Mario Testino

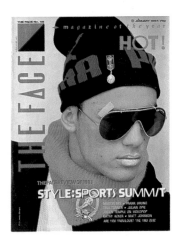  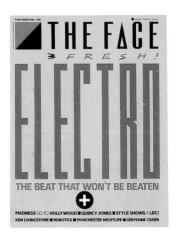 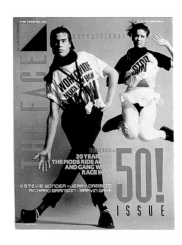

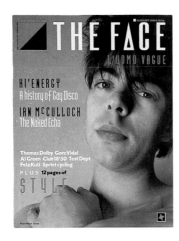

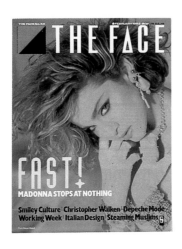

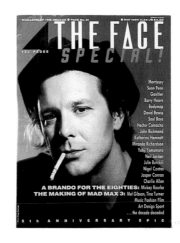

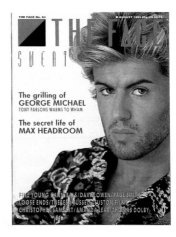

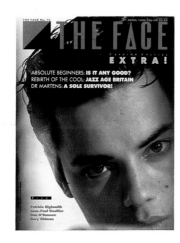

258. No.51,
July 1984,
Jamie Morgan

259. No.52,
August 1984,
Steve Tynan

260. No.54,
October 1984,
Greg Gorman

261. No.55,
November 1984,
Jamie Morgan

262. No.57,
January 1985,
Mike Laye

263. No.58,
February 1985,
Steve Meisel

264. No.61,
May 1985,
Greg Gorman

265. No.64,
August 1985,
Neil Kirk

266. No.65,
September 1985,
Tony Viramontes

267. No.68,
December 1985,
Pierre Hurel

268. No.69,
January 1986,
Jean Paul Goude

269. No.70,
February 1986,
Nick Knight

270. No.71,
March 1986,
Cindy Palmano

271. No.72,
April 1986,
Jamie Morgan

272. No.75,
July 1986,
Andrew Macpherson

273. No.76,
August 1986,
Robert Erdmann

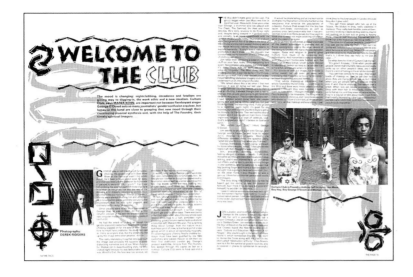

274. **Culture Club spread,** *The Face,* **No.28, August 1982**
275. **Malcolm Garrett profile,** *The Face,* **No.23, March 1982**
276. **Heaven 17 feature,** *The Face,* **No.24, April 1982**

Brody's design on the Culture Club and Malcolm Garrett pages shows an extension of hand-rendered elements, achieving vitality and movement. He introduced the typographic signposting that was later to emerge as the central feature. Heaven 17 required a more modular treatment – this was also a rare example of where the photograph was manipulated to illustrative effect.

'For a long time, the magazine was run from a small office in Soho. Visitors would come to the room in Broadwick St. expecting to find a large operation with plush offices. *The Face* was produced for the people who worked on it – the content of the magazine happened to collude with other people's interests, and it was then taken up by the media because they thought it was an easy way for them to obtain access to what was happening. Whether it was happening or not, it was taken as the truth. As far as the design was concerned, people were then unable to separate the dynamism I was trying to achieve with the style movement and advertising's pastiche of it.

'We wanted to bring a strong element of quality control that had to be seen all the way down the line. The magazine is put together during production week at a place in Kilburn in north-west London, where in one building there's a typesetter, a small editorial office, an artwork department and all the film origination for the printing plates. It was a well worked out system, but it needed to be: I had only 1½ hours to design a four-page feature. I didn't have to paste up the artwork myself because the planning was all done on pencil-layout grids, but this had the drawback that I would never see exactly how the photographs would work with the type until the magazine was printed. I was turning around 40 pages in as many working hours: it was necessary to have a full design team, but this was not financially possible. Within this short time, I'd probably have to draw up headline typefaces, which would be photocopied and lined-up very quickly. When I look at magazines that have the luxury of time (and most have a three-month lead time for features) and see how badly they can be put together, I find it frustrating to think that people would criticise *The Face* on the same basis.'

'Very often people will see a headline in *The Face* and say "we want that".'
(Dennis Collins, manager at Cogent Typesetters, Kilburn, quoted in *Lithoweek Supplement*, 23 October 1985).

'There were times when I felt that my work had been ripped off so much that I didn't want to make any new statement on the page whatsoever. I had initially developed hand-drawn lettering because it couldn't be so easily reproduced, and the first alphabet that I did was very geometric, austere and non-emotive. It was like a typeface from the 1930s, fascistic in a sense, and I was using it to comment on the state of the nation as I saw it. I was trying to pinpoint in the most graphic terms the parallel between what had happened in the Thirties, and the situation in the Eighties: the divided nation, the class division, the economic recession, and a highly authoritarian government.

'All the countless imitators of *The Face* haven't copied us only because of its success. The mentality of youth culture – 'to be young is good' – has arisen out of a much deeper division in society. Look at the trendy young couple shown in advertisements waltzing from one cashpoint machine to another.'

'Only the polythene bags tell you this is the 1980s, not the 1930s. To observe distinctly "modern" poverty in the River Streets you need to look for what was once expected and only briefly or never gained: telephones, a Sunday joint of meat, a hi-fi, warmth in winter, holidays, a night at the pictures, an outing anywhere. On Merseyside I am always struck by the bizarre billboards which exhort the young to buy £20-a-bottle French brandy, to smoke cigarettes out of a packet that looks like a gold brick, to talk to "the listening bank", to eat colourfully packaged junk, to take holidays in the Caribbean and to drive "Supercat", a Jaguar car worth more than £20,000. These are scattered, mysteriously, as if to taunt.'
(John Pilger, *Heroes*, Jonathan Cape, 1986)

'The car advertisements that say "better by design" are carefully letter-spaced not as a good example of design, but in order to signify design in the most vampiric sense. Punk was about using your self-expression against a culture you couldn't afford. I wanted to continue this in a different way. I took the manipulative language of advertising, street signs, and other information language and used them in a context where normality does not neutralise our awareness of them, isolating elements which tell you what to do and how to think, thereby uncovering them. Multinational organisations abduct colours for their corporate logos

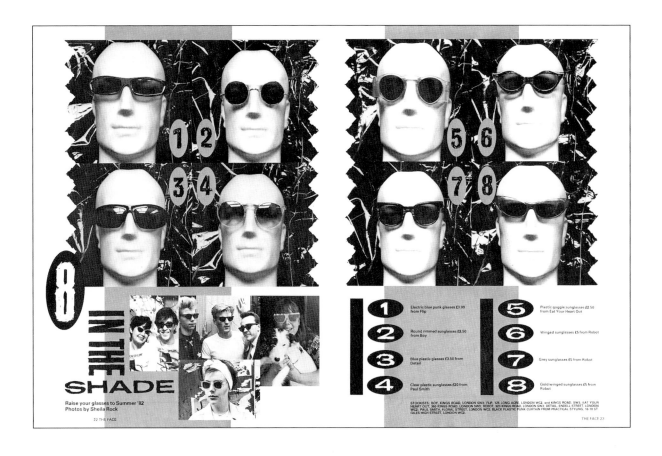

'I don't think Neville had to persuade me that much to run the type vertically on the cover. There were people on other magazines who sniffed at it, and then within six months there were vertical headlines everywhere you looked. There was a period when Neville tried to persuade me to run the logo on the side: I think August Darnell was the first one. I was very wary of it because of the effect it had on the news trade. They didn't like it. In some ways, having the logo on the side if the magazines are overlapped means that you can read it better; but for every newsagent who does that, there are others who put them underneath each other. Side logos didn't lower sales though, but we kept getting reps' reports saying "I don't mind if you do this, but don't keep changing".' (Nick Logan).

277. 'In the Shade', *The Face*, **No. 27, July 1982**
The hand-drawn approach has become more structured, a system of classification which was overstated to highlight the content. Typefaces are contrasted by their use at different angles, moving the eye around the information.

278. 'Odeon', *The Face*, **No. 27, July 1982**
In this layout, the photographs are paramount. The geometric type was an updating of 'Odeon' style.

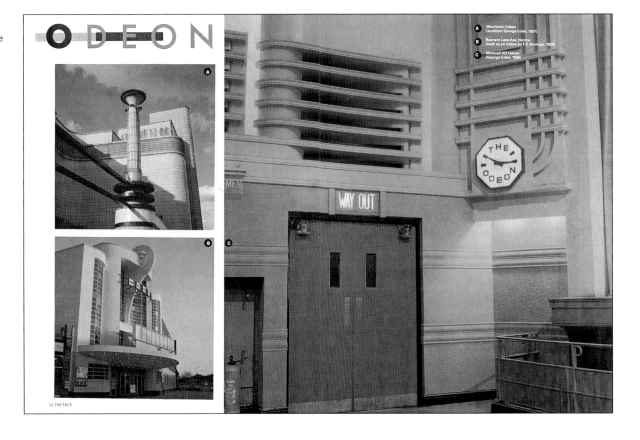

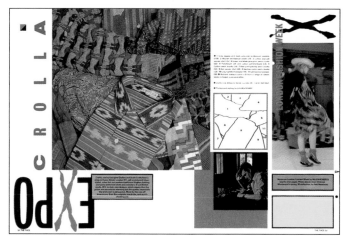

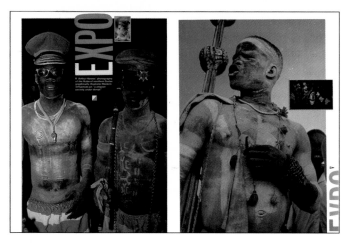

279. 'Workwear', *The Face*, No.30, October 1982
280. Expo on Scott Crolla, *The Face*, No.32, December 1982
281. Expo on Nubian tribesmen, *The Face*, No.34, February 1983
282. Cristina spread, *The Face*, No.32, December 1982
283/284. 'The Art of Jean-Paul Goude', *The Face*, No.28, August 1982

'Workwear' shows the first use of wide-spaced type in such a prominent fashion. All the typographic elements form an interlocking unit, so that information has to be read from all sides. Brushstrokes replace hand-rendered type. Against magazine convention, photographs were bled off the page, and to confound this, *The Face* 'flag' is used as a typographic element to reinforce the corporate identity of the magazine, also functioning as a structural marker similar to those used on the corner of buildings under construction. As usual, the structure is the primary element of the design.

JULY 1983 75p

EIRE £1.05 (INC. VAT)

THE FACE

NO HIDING PLACE ◆

NEW ORDER

EXCLUSIVE ◆

FILA, PRINGLE, LACOSTE

The ins and outs of High Street fashion

ART ON THE RUN

Colleges in Crisis: SHOCK REPORT

BILLY CONNOLLY BITES BACK

+ D·TRAIN · TERRY HALL · KENNETH ANGER
TRACEY THORN · SATURDAY NIGHT ON
RUSSIAN TV · HORROR · ROBERT WYATT

STEPHEN MORRIS OF NEW ORDER BY KEVIN CUMMINS

285. New Order cover, *The Face*, No.39, July 1983
It was thought that New Order were not recognisable enough to the general public to act as cover stars, so a different approach was needed. Brody therefore gave the photo of New Order's Stephen Morris a radical crop, helped further by the use of italic emphasis. This break with convention was subsequently chosen as 'Cover of the Year' in the 1983 Magazine Publishing Awards.

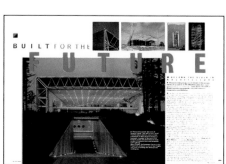

286. 'Built for the Future', *The Face*, No.34, February 1983
'I didn't use a Grotesque type so that I could dictate a style in typography. I used it because it best suited my purposes.'

287. Expo, *The Face*, No.34, February 1983

105

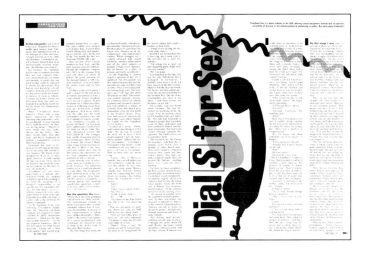

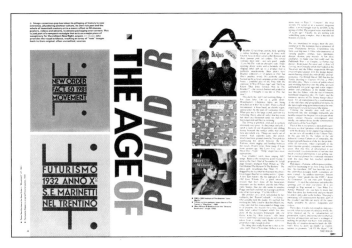

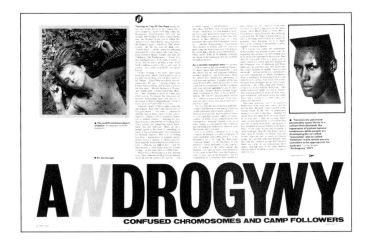

288. 'Dial S for Sex', The Face, No.44, December 1983
Small bars were used between each column of text to break up the solid copy, a codification in line with the content. The telephones are otherwise engaged.

289. 'The Age of Plunder', The Face, No.33, January 1983
290. 'Androgyny', The Face, No.38, June 1983
Written by Jon Savage, both features needed a design that conveyed the divergent nature of the subject matter. Letters were italicised within the main headlines, with symbols drawn to indicate the start of the text and its content. In 'The Age of Plunder', the dropped capital was drawn to contrast with the design solutions alongside it. In 'Androgyny' the text sat above the headline, creating an uneasy sense of balance.

and call them their own, as William Burroughs pointed out. I wanted to turn advertising back on itself, and the people I particularly wanted to address were the people in control of the media. Problems arose when advertisers started to emulate the layout of The Face, so at times the situation became very confusing. The design strategy of the High Street is established on the basis that trends in modern culture are so transient that it is impossible to pin them down or subvert them, and most people take the safest option of believing this to be an absolute truth.

'I attempted to show that it was possible to confound people's expectations of change within a commercial context. When the changes did not match up to what people expected, The Face was slagged off. The implications of this are frightening — such negativity has become an instinctive reaction against anything that tries to challenge the norm, even when people want that normality to be upset.'

'I was experimenting with the concept of a corporate identity for a magazine, a personality that could retain a consistency but would be forever changing. It had to be entertaining — The Face worked on the idea that if you are entertained at a primary level, then that will carry information through from the next level. I wanted to express the need to bring more life and humanity into our environment, with a greater sense of responsibility towards the way we design things. I was trying to say "things must be challenged". In my understanding of the mechanics of culture, The Face was not entirely successful because it simply became another set of ground rules for a new generation of designers. This wasn't the point. I wanted other people to challenge The Face, not to copy it, and I wanted to establish a strong dialogue. The Face was a catalyst for this argument — how can design bring a greater dynamism to the content, now that we live in a predominantly visual age? In many ways, The Face's commercial success took the impetus out of this. The problem is, when you challenge yourself — which is then taken to be The Face's ability to change its own style whenever it suited it — people never thought there could be a valid reason for making the change. Because some of the ideas behind The Face were so strong, the media's transposition of the magazine's success forced people into a corner where the easiest choice was to adopt the style — people had no option but to ignore what was really happening because the information was being presented to them second-hand. I was pointing out the means to a way of thinking and a way of working, not the solution. My work was a personal response to what I saw happening at large, but people only picked up on the surface effects. When the government was promoting monetary considerations as being more important than social welfare, and the culture as a whole was re-promoting surface values in a big way (particularly through the film and record industries), it led to the collision which is now "Success Culture".

'The creative process is about absorbing that initial stage and then, after that process, proceeding to react intuitively and to use the craft that you have developed. People don't do that. It never enters their soul. It always remains outside — they see something, they transfer it, and they never go through the process of internalising. Most design at the moment seems to hold no personal meaning to its exponents beyond its price-tag and promise of Culture. The commercial world is as responsible for this as individual designers — they need the work. You should not confuse this financial imperative with your true intentions, and simply become a prostitute to market forces.'

291/292/293. *Opposite:* **Contents page, The Face** No. 37, May 1983; **Annabella feature, The Face** No. 33, January 1983; **Review of 82, The Face** No. 33, January 1983
The scaffolding goes up for the next stage.

294. Nicolas Roeg feature, The Face, No. 38, June 1983
'The Face Interview' at this time had an adaptable generic style which used Albertus as the main headline together with Helvetica Bold Extended in a bar as the 'slug'. The early development of punctuation devices established a secondary grid structure.

295. Prince spread, The Face, No. 38, June 1983
Abstract shapes formed a crown over the headline whose words grouped together as if this were the only space allowed for them. Italics and a spot grey were used for emotive punctuation.

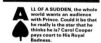

THE STYLE COUNSEL

● The State of the Nation's dress by Paul Weller

● Text by Lesley White: Photography Jill Furmanovsky

THE
STYLE
COUNSEL

"I SUPPOSE PEOPLE find it difficult to penetrate me," offers the pale young man in the white mac, "they're not sure whether I'm really deep or there's nothing there. I dunno myself." Most people his age wouldn't share this reluctance to describe Paul Weller, whether or not they'd met him or even listened to his songs. His reputation goes before, or rather *instead* of him, making him someone you just know about, have an opinion on.

Reluctant hero to a generation of sensitive suburban youth, Weller never demonstrated the obvious charisma of other teen idols. Articulate but never eloquent, he could almost have been any working class Woking boy – a quality that made him seem totally authentic, easy to both idealise and identify with. There *is* something very convincing about the man, an intensity that demands

24 THE FACE

respect. To his small circle of friends he is, simply, "the main man"; to the fanatically loyal Jam fans Weller walks on water. Quite a few people, however, wish he'd drown.

Always depicted as unsmiling, often accused of rigid dogmatism, the prospect of meeting this "spokesman for a generation" and "angry young man" (clichés breed clichés) was daunting. Moreover the challenge of not simply augmenting the dusty pile of "exclusive" interviews that all end up saying the same thing (being Paul Weller is a worthy but serious business) made wild invention an attractive proposition. Happily, it didn't come to that.

With one mythically successful chapter of his story completed and a fresh one begun with The Style Council, there was plenty of brand new ground and Weller covered it optimistically and light hearted. Even when I interrupted his work at Polydor studios two

days later to nervously report a faulty tape recorder and ask him to repeat the ordeal, he acquiesced, laughing. Perhaps I caught him on a good day (but twice?), perhaps the easy self-irony is newly learnt . . . either way, to set the record straight, his humour was never in doubt.

The video for "Speak Like A Child", the Style Council's debut single, proves the point. It has Weller and a group of friends attired in ludicrous Sixties gear romping through the Malvern Hills in an open-top bus: very Cliff circa '65 and very silly. At one point Weller recomposes that well known earnest expression . . . and the real Paul, watching beside me, laughs out loud at his own pathos.

That well documented concern with words like *honesty* and *dignity* still informs much of what he says but the austere puritanism I'd anticipated turned up as a relaxed confidence, the pragmatism of one who knows what he's

---

SOME
*GUYS
HAVE·ALL·THE
HITS

It's hard to be a superstar in today's tough musical world. Caught for a long time between ever-changing trends, ROBERT PALMER finally found his blue-eyed soul after a good deal of searching. Several glasses of Smirnoff later, the Northern rock'n'blues shouter was domiciled in Nassau and holidaying in Paris, where no-one was going to judge his music just by the cut of his clothes.

● Text Lesley White Photographs Jill Furmanovsky

"I'VE ALWAYS *LOATHED* THIS rock 'n'roll life style, you know," mused Robert Palmer in a sumptous hotel bedroom somewhere near the Champs Elysee. He went on to describe himself as an introvert who's overcome shyness, a pragmatist who's essentially romantic – with a personal book of dreams to prove it – and an ardent adversary of pride, vanity and narcissism.

When you're expecting to meet a man whose cynicism is as dry as his vodka-martinis, that kind of talk is very confusing. And in the record industry's market-place, where the stronger the image the more chance of trading it for some success, Palmer bemuses his public

and certainly his press by seeming to be both hedonistic playboy and dedicated "muso". His permanent residence abroad only compounds the enigma.

A name that's been around for 15 years, that's been used as index of both professionalism and plagiarism, and that's been dumped in as many musical bags as there are labels available, Palmer is as "misunderstood" as the next artist. That's the price he's paid – along with a poor singles record and a lot of stick – for not trying hard enough at self-promotion. Looking at him is seeing a well preserved piece of rock history; if he's kept the wrinkles at bay, the old clichés he embo-

dies are harder to smooth out. As the good-looking, urbane and inveterate bon viveur, Palmer has fooled and angered many. It's easy to locate the source of his unpopularity in his own myth; living the life of Riley and sunshine on funky Nassau, rolling off the beach and into Compass Point to knock out the odd album before the evening aperatif, disrespectful of British trends and other people's hard times; making 'every Habitat home should have one' records for people who stack their glossy covers under the Hockney prints and live lives like his songs: stylised vignettes of being in love or despair with enough money and nice clothes to do it with panache.

THE FACE 37

---

296. 'The Style Counsel', *The Face*, No.36, April 1983
297. Robert Palmer, *The Face*, No.35, March 1983

Headlines curved and fell out of true line at this stage, sometimes to form an emblematic design, and at others to create a literal movement where the eye had to follow the words and their shape. The punctuation alignment was by now ridiculous – a filing system for all the graphic information. Brody used slab serif type to offset the sans serif headlines, in the case of Paul Weller mixing typefaces in the same word for the first time. The Robert Palmer photo was bled off the foot of the page and cut to an angle at the top so as to enhance the movement in the photo, and to reinforce the emblematic quality of the main headline.

298. 'Lawyers, Guns and Money', _The Face_, No.45, January 1984
Brody decided upon a typographic treatment to articulate a feature about the music business — no photographs were to hand. The guiding idea was compression, and an exclamation mark sets off the text.

299. Tina Turner spread, _The Face_, No.45, January 1984

300. Simple Minds, _The Face_, No.48, April 1984
301. Carmel, _The Face_, No.41, September 1983

Brody introduced a softer and more sympathetic type style to allow photographs more space (contrast fig.277). No one element stands out at the expense of another. The Simple Minds spread has an almost pharmaceutical, pastel quality to it, upset by the ambiguous S+M logo. With Carmel, a strong vertical type column gives the photograph a stronger focal point, with the punctuation from the headline to text suggesting the automatic A to B of waking up in the morning.

302/303/304/305. Review columns, _The Face_; 1983/1984
Abstracted shapes were printed beneath the main copy to give emphasis to an otherwise flat page. Together with the vertical headline, the 'undercoat' provided a recognisable format.

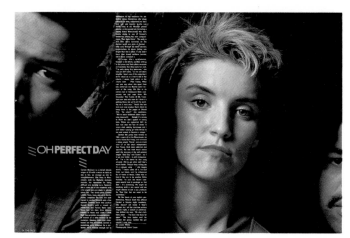

306. New Order feature, *The Face*, No.39, July 1983
The logo to the left of the headline is a further extension of the concept of corporate symbolism, with the photograph creating a sense of downward movement.

307. Mel Gibson, *The Face*, No.42, October 1983
The symbol and type were shot completely out of focus. A three-sided box isolated all the introductory information without totally enclosing it, though the text was unsuccessfully given a border in an attempt to treat it as raw information.

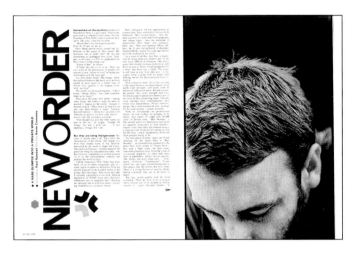

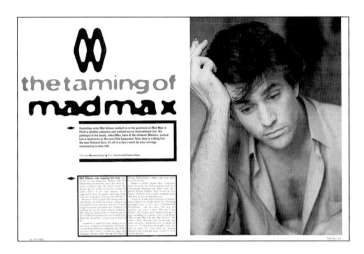

308. Jean-Paul Gaultier, *The Face*, No.46, February 1984
Typefaces were used that undermined the 'taste' that *The Face* represented. Corporate logos were, by now, the punctuation.

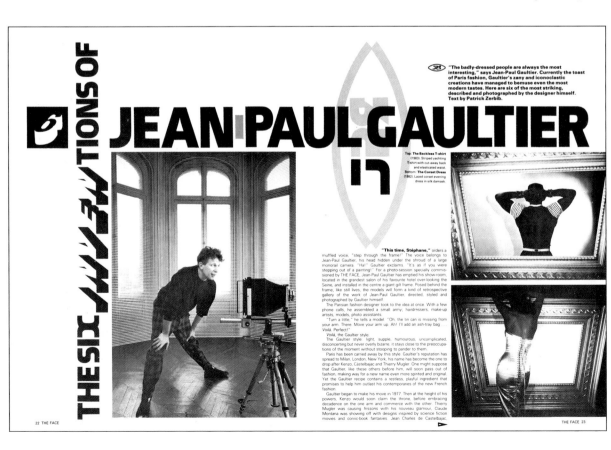

SKID ROMEO

Robert Elms travelled to East LA in search of the almost mythical Tom Waits, owner of a bad liver and a broken down Volvo . . .

When you ring Tom Waits you get an answerphone, a short burst of congas and a voice that drawls sleepily: "This is Tom, I'm at the beach." But there's no beach near his home in the Barrio and like as not he's sitting listening to your message, deciding whether to give you a burst of the live performer. Tom Waits is a famously private person; the Barrio is in east Los Angeles.

Waits is also a professional enigma. Despite ten years worth of bitingly intelligent, funny, dramatic music; despite album after album of the most essentially American songs white America has to offer, he's still no more than a goateed curio. If you're a fan he's a myth, if you're not he's a nobody. From where I stand Mr Waits is the only possible reason to leave the highly developed civilisation of Manhattan and head for the soporific wilds of the far west.

Before leaving the island I popped into Island. Waits, so long on WEA, is now one of Chris Blackwell's boys. "Swordfishtrombone" is his first solo album for three years, and I sat in an office and listened. After two sides of a TDK I was even more excited about the prospect of meeting the man. Tom has moved to a new motel, the Edward Hopper painting has become an Orson Welles picture. Oriental, disturbing, merry-go-round music with Hammond organ, electric guitar, tom-toms, chimes, bagpipes and a series of dark, tantalising scenarios sketched by a master storyteller. It's a soundtrack to a sad, unmade movie. Ben Gazarra should play the lead.

LA airport is in turmoil. The threat of next year's Olympics has turned it into a chaos of cement mixers and never-ending diversions. You may get lost in the airport, but you'll never even locate the city. "A city with all the personality of a paper cup" Raymond Chandler called it. I think he also said it was "seventy-two suburbs in search of a city". You can bet they never found it. Los Angeles doesn't really exist.

LA is a great big freeway, if you haven't got a car you can't live, if you have there's little worth living for. It's always hot and the scenery's very pleasant but you can drive for hours without hitting anything more exciting than housing estates, incredibly expensive housing estates. Hollywood's just a memory of a sign, a shadow on a hill populated by Californians. Californians are a breed together, united by the fact that they all wear shorts and all talk suntanned nonsense. When I told the girl at the car-hire company that I was there to interview a musician she was genuinely excited. When I told her it was Tom Waits she was genuinely disappointed.

"I like the ocean, but I don't feel very compatible with the type of people who are attracted to it" – Tom Waits.

To get from a hotel on Sunset Boulevard to the Travellers Rest Cafe you get on the Hollywood Freeway and keep going east. LA's east end is where they keep the 'wet-backs', all the poor illegal Mexican immigrants who've crossed the Rio Grande in order to sit on doorsteps and ride around in old cars that scrape the road.

Tom Waits and his wife are the only white people on their block, but there's seven catholic churches and the best chilli in the world. Round the corner is the Travellers, a Honduran diner with grey net curtains, a blackened plastic chandelier and a large black and white TV in the corner. When Tom walked in he looked just like his photos, just like one of his songs.

For a start he does talk with that voice. It may have been affected at one time, but there's no doubt that it's now the only voice he has. A lot of the time it's a low gruff whisper, barely audible above the baseball pouring out of the corner. The TV couldn't possibly be turned down so we paid for a couple of beers and left. We conducted the interview in his battered, maroon Volvo parked out on the strip.

"This street's great, every day there's a wedding or a funeral. The weddings are like processions, motorcades of late Fifties automobiles with huge Kleenex chrysanthemums strung across them. The men all wear lime-green tuxedos and the girls are straight of the top off a cake."

Tom Waits doesn't like doing interviews, but he's certainly no slouch at them either. Dragging me down to the tawdry glamour of a ghetto was a sweet move. Parked outside Los Quangos bar a vibrant, siren punctuated Latin hustle is going on all around us. There's a mariachi band in the bar and a stream of macho, low-rider Romeros wasting away the night. Tom Waits is younger than you expected, not far past thirty. My guess is that

44 THE FACE

THE FACE 45

309. Tom Waits, *The Face*, No.41, September 1983
310. Brian Eno, *The Face*, No.42, October 1983
The 'TW' logo is used as an anchor with an 'O' of the mixed-type headline giving further weight to the low text positioning. The headline for Eno was set in a particularly unattractive typeface that became usable through its treatment as no more than a structural element, strengthened by the two crosses.

ENO

ONLY THE SMALL SURVIVE

One of the vital musical innovators of the Seventies, Brian Eno now inhabits a curious world. He lives in 'medieval' Manhattan, where he gambles on the stock market and works with esoteric concepts that may just turn out to be mainstream. Oddball, erudite, unpredictable, his views are a constant challenge. Right now he can't stand rock videos . . .

Interview **Dave Rimmer** ◆ Photographs **Derek Ridgers**

A few years back I saw a film about Simone de Beauvoir. It consisted mostly of the talking (more precisely: philosophising) heads of herself and Jean-Paul Sartre. She was ageing elegantly; he – it was shortly before he died – an apparent physical wreck but still remarkably articulate. They discussed all sorts of weighty matters. What stuck, though, was the comic if slightly macabre sense of having watched two disembodied, characterless *brains* that did nothing but spout insights and which had simply been wheeled into proximity to interact for our entertainment.

Forgive my digression. The point is that interviews with Brian Eno – often consisting largely of direct quotes – frequently leave a similar, here-we-have-a-purely-intellectual-being impression. It's a classic "egghead" image, probably given a subliminal boost by pictures of his gently receding hairline. The reasons for this are obvious enough. He's a good talker whose usually refreshingly oblique perspectives are interesting and eminently quotable with a minimum of editing. "The reason I like to do interviews," he once said, "is it's a discipline for me. I can think out things that I wouldn't articulate otherwise."

It's also probably because the straight quote is the best way to cope in print with a man whose ideas – whether he's talking about video, evolution, his life in New York, the adolescent obsessions of most rock critics, the psycho-acoustical space of music or just telling a joke – constantly cross-refer and loop back on themselves.

There's a property of holograms: if you shatter one and look at a single fragment, you still see the whole image, only fuzzier. A good Eno quote is a bit like that.

And one other possible reason. Since most critics don't seem to know what to do with the "ambient" music he's mostly concerned himself with since abandoning the structures of rock, they probably find his talk easier than his work. This came up in the interview when I asked him what he considered the most astute, and the stupidest things ever said about him. To the latter he chuckled: "Most of the things written in the *New Musical Express*". The first he wanted time to think about, and was courteous enough to ring me from his holiday in Northumberland the following week with a list too long to quote in full. One was something Robert Wyatt once said to him (later to be incorporated in "Oblique Strategies" – the pack of aphoristic cards he and Peter Schmidt designed to be consulted at random in considering a problem): "You commit yourself to what you're left with". Another was what he could remember of a quote from WB Yeats:

"All empty souls tend toward extreme opinions. It is only in those who have built up a rich world of memories and habits of thought that extreme opinions affront the sense of probability."

One such opinion being the attitude of *NME* critics he was jibing at earlier, an "atmosphere" that fuels his reluctance to come back to England: "The idea that contemporary music is supposed to be something assertive and 'from the streets'; that if it isn't that, it's crap or pretentious. If it isn't made by people who wear leather jackets and take Quaaludes or whatever it is now, then it can't be authentic. In my experience the people who say this are always middle-class critics who never went through that and idealise this fictional notion."

From the streets, Eno's current work is not. In the "Mistaken Memories Of Manhattan" videos it was drifting across mysterious roof tops; on his last LP, the excellent "On Land", it was experimenting with a sense of landscape based around memories from his Sussex childhood. The music on his current LP, "Apollo", was composed to accompany a selection of NASA archive footage (soon to see the light of day in a film by Al Reinert) all the way to the moon.

Eno has described his ambient work as "figurative". Uneventful enough to serve as soothing background, it can also be eerily evocative if approached more intently. Much of "On Land" was built around vague "animal noises". For "Apollo" the figurative approach presented a problem: there is no noise in space. One series of pieces is anchored in a shimmering sound he invented to "describe" stars ("I was pleased with that one"); another around gentle slide-guitar playing, Eno having discovered that all the Texan astronauts took country and western tapes up there with them. The results bear as much resemblance to conventionally "spacy" music as "On Land" does to the music in Wimpy Bars.

A key intention of Eno's is to inject a sense of place into his music. He recently took this further with a massive video installation in Japan involving 36 monitors – some linked, some individual – and a total of 72 speakers dotted about the room. Each would be repeating its own sound or image, all at different lengths to provide a gentle looping and changing. A selection of comments from the visitors' book:

"What a fantastic space! I felt like I was floating."
"I felt like I was being fed some kind of food at a zoo."
"It reminded me of my home town."
"I saw a couple making love in the zone and I was very jealous."
"I miss Eno's rock and roll."

Like most people who visit Japan, Eno was impressed and intrigued. His New York studio was recently cleaned out by burglars, convincing him it's time to move. Maybe to Tokyo.

Eno has always explored interesting side-tracks rather than follow the straight and narrow path of least resistance. In the process he's been credited with, or blamed for, any number of things. The introduction of African sensibility into pop consciousness via Talking Heads, for example. In particular, his pioneering synthesizer work and advocacy of the studio-as-creative-tool have certainly contributed to the ever more dreary electronic pop boom. But then, if people want to follow him down one of those side-tracks, and then the music business contractors move in, pave the thing over and turn it into a horrible 3-lane motorway, that's hardly his fault.

Hardly anyone as yet has followed him in his ambient excursions, although I think he'd dearly like them to. Just as he'd like more music and video practitioners to avoid the easy option and indulge in the mix of playfulness, careful thought and random intuition he's developed into a total working method.

14 THE FACE

15

BEUYS⁺ ADVENTURES

By Anthony Fawcett and Jane Withers

Joseph Beuys is at once the most influential and controversial artist to emerge from post-war Germany. His cathartic presence has resounded far beyond the narrow confines of the art world. He is a radical opponent to convention and a catalyst for new developments in all fields of contemporary life. He has been acclaimed as a father figure by a whole spectrum of artists — from the young painters exhibited at the Berlin *Zeitgeist* exhibition to the German music scene. He was founder of the German Students Party and the Organization for Direct Democracy and an inspirational force behind Germany's influential ecological party, the *Greens*. It is hard to imagine anyone who could equal the energy Joseph Beuys brings to such a multitude of concurrent projects. His favourite slogan is: "Everyone can be an artist . . . All life is art."

311. Joseph Beuys, *The Face*, No.40, August 1983
312. Cabaret Voltaire, *The Face*, No.40, August 1983
Brody arranged the Beuys layout as a form of typographic performance — the headline is weighted to enable the opening text to be wide-spaced; Beuys' own symbol, *Hauptstrom*, and the photo-caption beneath it bring extra vitality. 'Life Is A Cabaret' is made readable by its bold 'C': the upside down 'LIFE', however, is the real headline, creating with the photograph an almost abstract magazine layout.

LIFE IS A CABARET

By Anthony Denselow
Photos Peter Ashworth

313. Jamie Reid, *The Face*, No.42, October 1983
Brody decided to contrast original Punk graphics with the headline's typographic anarchy — by justifying its letters to the same height, this was carefully regulated to highlight the feature's content, contrasting Punk with a non-Punk format.

314/315. 'Europe' feature, *The Face*, No.43, November 1983
The 'E' of 'Europe' is not a letterform, a sign towards later experimentation in *The Face* where words were formed out of symbols.

316. 'The Perfect Beat', *The Face*, No.42, October 1983
The large logo suggested the enclosed space of a discotheque. The headline bled onto the previous page to close in on an advertisement.

'When I set up *The Face*, I initially tried to cost it without advertising revenue; again, it was a reaction to the other magazines I'd worked for. But things were difficult financially and I realised that I needed the advertising. I picked up a few, but we didn't get a proper ad. department until the 4th year.

I don't think we ever purposely tried to influence the look of an advert, but certainly, unintentionally, the magazine has had that effect. There were a few, much later on, that we turned away — and two double spreads, which I think we carried twice, that looked so horrid that we dissuaded the advertisers when they came to re-book. Sometimes you might get someone phoning up, wanting a rate card, and they'd be selling the kind of mail-order stuff you get in the back of the *NME*. We'd just let the inquiry die a natural death, but there wasn't a lot turned away.' (Nick Logan, July 1987).

'In the European issue, I decided to subvert the European success in all forms of art by using Ancient Mexican symbolism. This undermining factor was trying to pinpoint Europe's colonial plunder, and how easily it had become a tradition — I don't think many people, or even *The Face*, realised this side to the design.'

HOLIDAYS IN HELL

RIO DE JANEIRO
The Moleques or 'beach rats' of Rio. Aged between 12 and 15, they spend their days hunting tourists and gambling away the proceeds. If you don't have a Rolex or a Walkman, they'll take your trainers instead

You've trekked across the Himalayas, taken a train to Peking, gone topless at St. Tropez. You've been everywhere, seen everything and done it all twice. You're bored, jaded, blasé — but still restless. You want more than just a cheap holiday in someone else's misery. Next year, try Soweto. Your pass will be valid until ten pm, after which you're on your own. Or Beirut, where you can sunbathe as the rockets fly overhead. Or how about Rio, or the Bronx, or even Amsterdam — all places that guarantee an extra *frisson*. We tell you how to get there, and how to die there . . .

● By Pierre Hurel/AWAKS

THE FACE **39**

317. '**Holidays In Hell**', *The Face*, **No.53, September 1984**
A right-hand page opener that clearly shows the hallmarks of Brody's design. The symbol at the head of the page relates to a code on a film pack (the rays of the enclosed sun were in fact cutting blades). A curved edge to its border creates a downward movement to the text information. The reversed-out 'E' of the headline hints at what Brody describes as 'the hidden world' behind typography, where a roman letterform is made to seem an italic. The directional 'bullet' is exaggerated in size to announce its change from the triangle used hitherto.

● An Easter miracle: the resurrected Chad returns to base

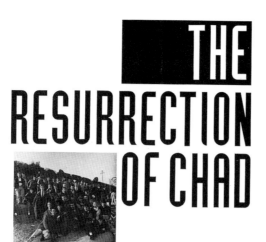

THE RESURRECTION OF CHAD

For two days the town slept uneasily, anticipating events prophecied by dark whispers in the road-side inns. As the pilgrims gathered by their tents, huddled in Parkas, a hush fell on the East Coast. There was going to be trouble. The omens had been read in the popular press of 20 years past. Chad, the son of Mod, was dead. Roll away the scooters. Let the soul classics ring out. For on the third day, there occured a modernist miracle! Twenty years after the first Mod runs of the Sixties, THE FACE rides along with the Class of '84.

Twenty years ago the Easter weekend in Clacton was the coldest since 1884; on this April Saturday the weather is more clement. Rows of gleaming scooters, L-plates shimmering in the pale sunshine, line the sea front. Mildly curious, holiday makers stop to admire the more flamboyant ones and move on to the tawdry delights of a shingle beach and an overcrowded pier. The conservatory window of a dilapidated hotel displays a group of watery-eyed East Coast geriatrics watching for the first signs of bloody gang warfare. It's been 20 years, almost to the day, since the last memorable event in this quiet Essex resort – the original headline-hogging Mod versus Rocker battles of Easter '64.

"I like 'avin' 'em 'ere," says Mr Alf Lee, a youthful if toothless 77, "at least it makes some news in this old age pensioners town."

Outside another hotel further up the coast road the entire cast of Quadrophenia appear to be sipping cans of Special Brew, checking out old friends, catching up on news and greeting late arrivals with affable abuse as they burn gently into town. The incessant pill-sustained chatter spans the usual subjects: where they'll go to pose tonight, the run from London – a few recount roadside encounters with Hells Angels: "We don't fight with them any more" – and, for those camping on the primitive site allotted by the local council, the problem of getting a free shower. The canny, fastidious and better-heeled among them arrived yesterday to commandeer the town's limited bed & breakfast accommodation. Someone reckons there'll be 2,000 here by nightfall. Nobody's quite sure what to do next; nobody really minds.

The best scooters seem to belong to the boys in army greens and Doc Marten boots. "They're scooterists, not Mods," says an effete young man in a single-breasted blue suit, "make sure you get that." The scooterist on my left is in the Islington-based Angel Scooter Club which, he fancies, is second only to the revered scooter-skin club, The Brittania. He used to be a mod in '79 but he can't be bothered with the clothes these days. He needs every penny of his factory wage packet for beer, the baby his girlfriend's expecting any time now and spare parts. Blue Suit cringes.

Deciding he needs to buy some cigarettes, he tries to enter the hotel via a side door. Three old ladies inside see him coming and quickly bolt the door. He waits, smiling tolerantly. Eventually the bravest of the three opens the door to ask what he wants and, walking stick raised, tells him to go away. He shrugs and walks off.

As the lunch time bar closes Parkas, Fred Perries, Suede Jackets and Blazers drift half a mile up the road to the campsite on the edge of town, there to sleep, rescue crumpled suits from polythene bags and preen for the evening or simply ride in circles round the dirt track surrounded by 40 or so amateurish tents, enjoying freedom from the crash helmet law.

Words Lesley White ● Photography Steve Tynan

28 THE FACE / THE FACE 29

318. 'The Resurrection of Chad', The Face, No.50, June 1984
319. 'Role Over and Enjoy It!', The Face, No.53, September 1984
320. Thomas Dolby, The Face, No.52, August 1984

At this point in The Face's history, the magazine needed to re-establish its independent status and personality. In order to strengthen its identity and to counteract the increasingly frequent imitations, Brody decided to introduce a specially-drawn typeface – designed to be effective both for headlines and straplines (see figs.50/51/52/53).

'Neville always changes before I've quite finished with a typeface. So many of them are one-offs. It would annoy me that people would take up an idea that Neville had discarded, and because it was no longer in The Face, they would have free rein with it. Other people would look at it and think "that's a brilliant design" without knowing where it came from.' (Nick Logan).

role over ●AND ENJOY IT!

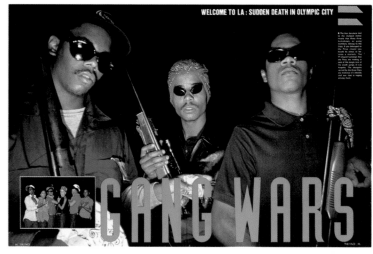

DC FREEZE

WELCOME TO LA : SUDDEN DEATH IN OLYMPIC CITY

GANG WARS

MERSEY BEAT

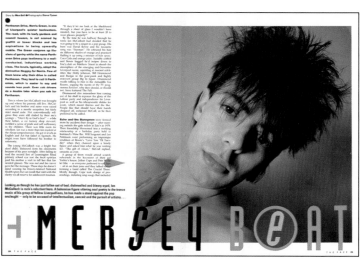

321/322. *Opposite:* **'DC Freeze'**, *The Face*, **No.60, April 1985**
323. 'Gang Wars', *The Face*, **No.50, June 1984**

'One of the things that we have always struggled to do is to get a good form of design for the documentary pieces. "Gang Wars" is very good for this kind of story. In a way, I think we lost it afterwards, and are still finding it a problem, really. You've got the weight and history of the colour supplement bearing down on you. It's difficult to find new formats for a reportage piece that don't detract from the seriousness of the story.'
(Nick Logan)

324/325. Ian McCulloch, *The Face*, **No.52, August 1984**
The typographic variation within the headlines was by this time streamlined, extending the idea of organic design and modular structure. In fig.325, a section of the headline articulates the continuation of the feature; another meaning emerges as a result of this abbreviation, perhaps defying the myth of a corporate Liverpool, where 'The Cavern' nightclub made famous by The Beatles is now a shopping arcade – built for a city currently suffering worse than most from poverty, bad housing and unemployment.'

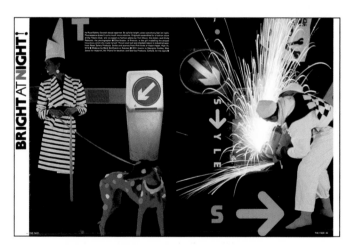

326/327/328/329. Various 'Style' spreads, *The Face*, **Nos. 39, 38, 48, 48, July 1983, June 1983 and April 1984**
'Style' replaced the word 'fashion' in *The Face* to concentrate upon an overall 'look' and 'feel'. Around this time the Stylist became as important as the Clothes Designer – one benefit, at least, was that the spreads were never constructed as if they were consumer catalogues.

ital style

330. 'Ital Style', *The Face*, No.58, February 1985
This spread marks the introduction of a new typeface (see fig.59) which is reversed out of block for emphasis. The previously exaggerated punctuation and directional devices have by now become less significant, the movement relying upon the direction of the design and type themselves.

THE glamourous life

● By Jeffrey Ferry

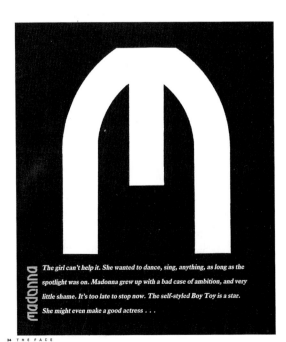

The girl can't help it. She wanted to dance, sing, anything, as long as the spotlight was on. Madonna grew up with a bad case of ambition, and very little shame. It's too late to stop now. The self-styled Boy Toy is a star. She might even make a good actress . . .

"MANIPULATING PEOPLE, THAT'S what I'm good at." Madonna says it matter-of-factly, and smiles. Her upper lip stretches taut across her wide mouth, her teeth flash, and she laughs. The laugh says she's making a joke, and you're not meant to believe it. But the eyes tell you to believe her. She is serious. She's a serious girl.

Madonna wants desperately to be a star. A big star. Having a Number One single and a Number Two LP in the US, as she did in December, is nowhere near enough. She got in trouble for saying on American TV that her ultimate goal was to rule the world. She says to me instead that it is "to stand next to God," and laughs. But I believe her.

There is something special about her. It has little to do with her singing, which is indifferent, nor her dancing, which is merely proficient, nor her fashion sense, which we can summarise best perhaps by saying she is a fast learner. It has something to do with the beauty and sexuality she radiates, but even more, it is the effect of her extraordinary personality. Madonna is a strange, uniquely American creation: on the outside she is all ambition and determination, raw will to succeed. But on the inside, like a grain at the centre of a pearl, is a strange and unexpected fragility. The tension between these two makes Madonna a fascinating, even irresistible character; one who, it is all too easy to believe, is destined for the success she craves.

Possibly she will do it as a pop star, you feel, but perhaps more likely, as an actress. And there are some people in New York who are saying she will be the next Marilyn Monroe . . .

"Madonna is a child-woman," says Maripol, her French-born clothes designer. "She is fun and joyful, but she is also a femme fatale. She is vulnerable – but then she's not that vulnerable. She's not tough exactly – but she'll survive through anything. She's a natural star. She is born to stardom."

WHAT SHE WAS BORN to, in fact, was a large lower-middle-class Italian-American family in industrial Detroit, Michigan. The Ciccones might have been a very happy family, if Madonna's mother hadn't died early on of cancer, tragically misdiagnosed by the doctors. Young Madonna was only seven at the time and her world was shattered. Her father couldn't cope with taking care of six children and holding down his engineering job, working on defence systems for the Chrysler Corporation, so the children were sent off to live with various relatives.

After several months of shuttling from relative to relative, Madonna's father hired a housekeeper and all the children were able to return home. But for Madonna there was no going back to the stability of earlier days. Her father went through a succession of housekeepers, none of whom Madonna remembers liking. He eventually married one of them, when Madonna was ten.

"My father's marriage was a surprise to us because we all thought he was going to marry someone else who looked very much like our mother, and we were rooting for her. She looked sorta like Natalie Wood, or that's what I thought she looked like when I was a child. But then suddenly he didn't marry her . . . I wasn't that fond of my stepmother. She was really gung-ho, very strict, a real disciplinarian."

Without getting excessively Freudian about it, it seems fair to say that Madonna's childhood experiences have a lot to do with the fragility and insecurity which Madonna exudes. But at the same time, she is a fighter. And the struggle to win the love she sought from her father, in competition with her stepmother and the seven other children in the house, turned the little girl into a very precocious young woman.

"From when I was very young, I just knew that being a girl and being charming in a feminine sort of way could get me a lot of things, and I milked it for everything I could."

The strict discipline of her Catholic school education reinforced Madonna's feelings of being lonely and unloved – she describes Catholicism as "dark, painful and guilt-ridden" – and responded by becoming an even more flamboyant attention-getter.

"I wanted to do everything everybody told me I couldn't do. I had to wear a uniform to school, I couldn't wear make-up, I couldn't wear nylon stockings, I couldn't cut my hair, I couldn't go on dates, I couldn't even go to the movies with my friends. So when I'd go to school I'd roll up my uniform skirt so it was short, I'd go to the school bathroom and put make-up on and change into nylon stockings I'd brought. I was incredibly flirtatious and I'd do anything to rebel against my father."

Her craving for attention led her into performing. At school, she was a cheerleader and a baton-twirler, but soon became more ambitious:

"Every chance to make up a little song and dance routine, I took advantage of it, and I always got standing ovations. Finally I decided to devote myself professionally to it. I started taking ballet classes with a really strict ballet teacher – he was very Catholic and 'you're beautiful'. He never said I'd make a great dancer, he just said 'you're very special'."

Dance and performing provided the outlet for her energies that she was seeking, and filled the voids she felt.

"I never had a group of friends in school. I kept to myself and did what I wanted to do. But it bothered me. I think I was lonely in lots of ways. And when I latched onto the dance

thing, I was with older and more sophisticated people. I felt really superior. I just felt that all this suffering that I felt for not fitting in is worth it – I don't fit in because I don't belong here. I thought, I belong in some special world."

MADONNA TALKS ABOUT THE development of her extrovert, showbiz 'sex-kitten' persona with an almost clinical detachment. It is as if she too is amazed that such a lonely little girl could grow such a rock hard outer layer of ambition. But grow it she did, and by her late teenage years, the determination to be a star utterly eclipsed everything else in her life.

I asked Madonna if, as a Catholic, she found it difficult deciding to lose her virginity.

"Oh no. I thought of it as a career move." Laughter – and again those wide eyes which refuse to let you take it as just another joke.

At 17 Madonna set off in search of her special world – she went to New York. "It was the first plane ride of my life. I didn't know anyone. I didn't have a place to stay, and I only had $35 in my pocket."

Times were rough at first. She moved around constantly, was often broke, and didn't really enjoy the dance schools she enrolled in. But she graduated to the world of rock'n'roll, sensing that it held out the best possibilities for stardom.

The story of her rise to fame has such a methodical inevitability, you'd think it was written in Hollywood. Indeed, Madonna's story would have made a far better film than the actual *Flashdance*. In New York she met a boy named Dan, who persuaded her to join his rock band and move in with him. He taught her to play guitar and write music. Then a boy named Steve, an old boyfriend from Detroit, whom she bumped into by chance in New York, inspired her to take her music in a disco direction, and to make some demo tapes.

Her next boyfriend introduced her to New York's thriving "new wave" nightclub scene. Madonna developed an interest in trendy fashion and became one of New York's "night people". She went to the trendy discos nearly every night, and told everybody she met that she wanted to be – was going to be – a big star.

It was in the NY clubs that she developed her own dress style, one which is still with her. Picture it as a wrestling match between the skimpiness of her garments with a stunningly excessive collection of jewellery, mostly in metal and rubber, much of it with a strong Catholic motif (crucifixes and rosaries in places which would give nuns apoplexy). The jewellery – from Maripolitan on Bleecker St. – is much the best bit, and you don't need to have the body of Madonna to wear it.

Mark Kamins, DJ at Danceteria, met her in

**331. Madonna, *The Face*, No.58.
February 1985
332/333. Andy Warhol, *The Face*, No.59,
March 1985**

The opening M of the Madonna spread was
turned upside down for the opening of the
Andy Warhol spread in the following issue,
even retaining part of the small photograph
of Madonna, bleeding off the edge of the
page. Although most people assumed this
layout to be a mistake or a joke, it was a
means of questioning Warhol's use of re-
usables. The repeated photographs added
weight to this. The headline set up a modular
system that further highlighted Pop Art's
premises and their unchallenged social
acceptability. The 'subtext' of the layout hints
at the sexual and public profile of Warhol.

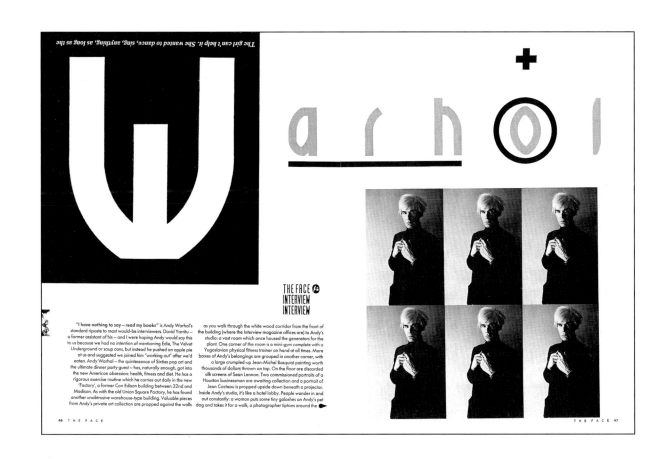

culture JUNCTION

At the crossroads of Rasta and Cockney stands Smiley Culture, with a wry line on both. He could have been a used car dealer. Instead he's become the first Fast Style MC in the pop charts. Can he survive reggae's latest craze?

Words Robert Elms ● Photographs Derek R.

ADRIENNE POSTA AND ALFIE BASS would still recognise Clapham Junction. They went *Up The Junction* in 1967 to make one of those grainy British comic-realist movies, and to this day the corner of South London that is so inappropriately known as Lavender Hill remains a fine example of inner city rot. It's the part of Clapham where the tubes don't go, unlike 'Clahm' Common it hasn't been gentrified by advertising and media folk and prettified by carriage lamps.

The Falcon on the corner by the market is a perfect reflection of Clapham Junction; old, solid and dour. There are gingham tablecloths and quiche pies in one corner in case any of the nearby nouves pop in for a glass of wine on their way to Arding & Hobbs, but the majority of the clientele is strictly Junction old and new. There's the auld fellows cradling pints of lager, with shiny arses on their suits and shiny noses on faces that haven't seen Ireland in too long. Then there's the young rude boys taking a Special Brew before crossing over to the Dub Vendor. That's Dub Vendor, home of Fashion Records, home of Smiley Culture.

Is it their prejudice or mine which makes it so difficult for a white non-believer to walk into one of those shops? Since the demise of Bob Marley reggae has become ghetto music once again, slunk back into its urban strongholds, back into Blues parties, and onto pirate radio, and back into dense and daunting little shops like the Dub Vendor. Most of the young attracted by reggae's militancy in the late Seventies have moved on to the fresh pastures of African music; Soca is far more viable all-round as party music. Recent reggae has simply passed the mainstream by because it is so impenetrable. No pop and little style, until Smiley Culture.

Taking "Police Officer" – only his second record – into the national pop charts and thus the nation's living rooms is a fine achievement by the 22-year-old Fast Style MC. As with its predecessor, the wonderful "Cockney Translation", young Mr Culture's new recital has a humour, a charm and a pertinence which has been so lacking in most recent self-righteous reggae. The old cliché about all reggae records sounding the same seems to have come true. They all have the sound of sufferation, but not Smiley Culture's.

"Reggae got into a phase of oppression, but people don't want to hear about things that are going to get them down. They don't want to know that they are going to burn in brimstone and fire."

SMILEY CULTURE'S REAL name, David Victor Emanuel, is the result of a mixed and divided marriage. Mum is South American and lives in South London, dad Jamaican and living in New York, flying search patrol helicopters for the NYPD. Baby David was born here, went there, and came back to be educated.

"I've been going to parties and rave-ups for as long as I've known myself," he remarks of his upbringing. The party-going was tempered with the Pentecostal church-going that most West Indian kids are forced to participate in. The

24 THE FACE

THE FACE 25

337/338. Contents pages, *The Face*, Nos. 58 and 59, February and March 1985
The use of the images by the Steaming Muslims complemented the new Contents logo (see figs. 75 to 81), with white space broken by the dynamic movement of the figure's curved line In the following issue, the contents logo melts into an indistinguishable mass, an alien monster in an issue of *The Face* called 'Killer' (see fig. 233).

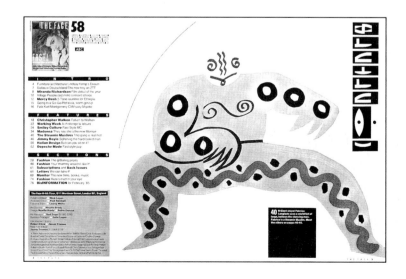

true west!

SAM SHEPARD

"You can either die like a dog or die like a man," concludes SAM SHEPARD. And if you figure in one of his plays, you have to bide your time in a Mescal-inspired desert of motels and bars. As an acclaimed playwright and actor, Shepard has brought back to life some rugged American myths. Is he the new Hemingway, or just the new Gary Cooper? By Blanche McCrary Boyd

SAM SHEPARD WAS EXPLAINING why he'd refused to be featured on the cover of *Newsweek*. "I think it's silly to become a cover story. You don't have to go out of your way to be a face that everybody sees."

He was dressed in his Sam Shepard uniform: faded jeans, worn boots, a leather belt with a big buckle, and a western shirt. His cowboy hat hung on the back of a chair.

The face he'd like to keep anonymous is lean and weathered, with high cheekbones and brown eyes that slant slightly. His hairline is receding from a widow's peak. Although he's not conventionally good-looking, his rough elegance is compelling.

Jessica's fame, he was saying, presents enough problems. When they drive cross-country, the Midwest is pretty good. They can go into truck stops and nobody pays attention. But as soon as they hit Colorado, around Denver, it starts. "Waitresses, people coming out of the goddamn kitchen to get autographs – so mainly we stick to truck stops in Nebraska and Kansas. We have a good time out there." He smiled, revealing a brown, broken front tooth.

In photographs he's usually fierce, and in movies he rarely shows his teeth, but in person Sam Shepard laughs easily and often, although those eyes have something raw behind them.

We were eating enchiladas at the Staab House, a discreet restaurant in one of Santa Fe's nicer hotels, where no waitress would dare intrude on Sam or Jessica. For most of the morning we'd been talking into a tape recorder, and I was surprised he accepted an invitation to lunch. His reason soon surfaced. "She's here somewhere. She's supposed to be in this restaurant, doing an interview of her own."

He craned his neck to see onto the restaurant's small upper level. "There she is."

I turned and glimpsed Jessica Lange, her hair dyed red for a Showtime/PBS taping of *Cat On A Hot Tin Roof*. She was deep in conversation. Her four-year-old daughter, Shura, sat in her lap. Sam stood up and waved, shouting, "Miss Lange! Miss Lange!"

SAM SHEPARD MAY BE THE BEST living playwright in America and a film actor of remarkable presence, but he is most noticeably a man in love. His conversation is full of references to Jessica Lange, their relationship, and her influence on his life.

They met in 1981, filming *Frances*, and have been involved off and on ever since. A year ago they bought a ranch outside Santa Fe and moved in together, along with Shura. They chose Santa Fe because Sam likes the desert, and his father lived here, and it is a good place to keep horses. He and Jessica both ride horses: Sam competes in rodeos and recently took up polo; Jessica jumps.

They are starting together in a new film called *Country*, which Jessica coproduced. Sam and Jessica play Gilbert and Jewell Ivy, a storybook farming couple who were high school sweethearts and even lost their virginity to each other. Jewell inherited land, Gil farmed it, they spawned three perfect children, always said grace before meals, went to church on Sunday, and everything went just great until Mother Nature and the American government joined hands to force the Ivys and all their neighbours into insurmountable debt.

Sam's relationship with Jessica has its own storybook quality. He made *Country* "because of her. We'd just gotten together, and she was all committed to this thing." The man who turned down *Newsweek* consented to this interview because Jessica wanted the film promoted. He's not convinced that promotion has any significance ("Either the film is good or it's not") but "I'm doing it for her." (Subsequent to my visit, Sam agreed to be photographed with Jessica for a fashion layout in *Vanity Fair*, presumably also "for her.")

Sam was comfortable with the character he played in *Country*. He grew up on an avocado ranch in California, was in the 4-H Club in high school, and, for his one year of college, majored in agriculture. He tends to stay away from roles that run counter to his sense of himself, especially in projects with Jessica. Her next film will be about Patsy Cline. "She wanted me to do this part, another one of these guys who's so screwed up he beats her up; she's the martyred woman and all. I just figured I didn't want to do that."

William Witliff wrote *Country* and co-produced it with Jessica. Production began with Witliff as director, but two weeks into the shooting, he was relieved of that assignment. "Jessica," Sam said, "just didn't like what she was seeing in the dailies. And that was flat it, you know? She should be a director. She's got a great eye."

The project was stranded on location in Waterloo, Iowa. Enter Richard Pearce, who had directed *Heartland*, a film about Montana immigrants in the early 1900s. "Sometimes," Sam said, sounding suspiciously like a publicist, "when a project is in crisis, and somebody comes in and just acts like he knows what he's doing, it's exactly what is needed. The project just takes *off*. Dick did a brilliant job of coming in and saving the thing."

Shura had wandered over to our table. She is angelic looking, a fantasy child with luminously blonde hair and clean, lovely features. She was wearing a white dress and carrying a tiny mermaid doll with long green hair. Shura's father is Mikhail Baryshnikov.

"Hello, Shura," Sam said gently, "have you had your lunch?"

Nodding, she climbed onto his lap. He put

THE FACE 23

---

339. **Sam Shepard**, *The Face*, No.59, **March 1985**
340. **Bob Hoskins**, *The Face*, No.60, **April 1985**

Shapes acted as the pivot for the layouts at this point. The Bob Hoskins spread was the first time that Brody shaped the text to suit the design, creating a greater architectural movement.

BOB HOSKINS

HE WOKE UP TO FIND HIMSELF IN REPERTORY ASKING "HOW D'YOU PLAY THIS GAME?"

the finsbury park empiricist

STOP ME IF YOU'VE HEARD THIS ONE...

No-one ever called Bob Hoskins pretty. The story goes that when he was a kid, growing up off the Holloway Road in North London, his mum once lost him. When she bewailed the fact that thieves had stolen him, his auntie quipped that with his angelic looks, "If they have taken him, I can tell you they'll soon fucking bring him back."

Those glinting eyes, that squidgy nose and piranha-like grin meant Hoskins was never going to be the new Michael Caine. The new Al Capone perhaps; but not a big movie star. Yet in 1978 when he appeared as the lead in Dennis Potter's TV musical *Pennies From Heaven*, the *Daily Mirror* went wild for this "leering charmer with a song in his heart."

And when he starred as the ruthless East End gangster Harold Shand in the movie *The Long Good Friday* he received the ultimate accolade: fan mail from the Kray twins.

It had been a long haul through a string of parts – all from the Madame Tussaud's of turpitude and villainy. He played Napoleon, Richard III and the malevolent Iago in *Othello*; he's been a rock'n'roll manager in *The Wall*, the scheming Machiavellian assassin Bosola in *The Duchess Of Malfi*, a bullying policeman in *The Honorary Consul*, even Ronnie Kray himself in *England, England*. The National Theatre cast him as Nathan Detroit in their *Guys And Dolls*, while Italian TV called on him to play Mussolini.

But when Francis Ford Coppola chose him to play Owney Madden, the real-life gangster clubowner of the Cotton Club, Hoskins knew he'd really made it. "New York," he'd always felt, "was like Dalston – only bigger." But there he was in the Big Apple, being courted by the elite as if he were some cockney reincarnation of Edward G. Robinson. He looked round at his drinking partners one night, and there were the faces of Al Pacino, Gene Hackman, Robert Duvall and Robert De Niro. Their aunties probably never thought they were pretty either.

THE CHEEKY CHAPPY
"You wouldn't think I was sexy to look at me, would you? Well, I 'ave a go, lady. I 'ave a go, don't I? I do. I 'ave a go..."
The Entertainer (1957) John Osborne

One of Bob Hoskins' earliest memories is visiting the old Finsbury Park Empire, his

THE FACE 21

341. Sting, *The Face*, No.63, July 1985
A new typeface was introduced to articulate a more classical feel to some of the pages (see fig.56). The photograph's border was kept within the spread for its impact, rather than bleeding off the edge of the page, as had been customary. The word 'Sting' appeared small and wide-spaced on the edge of the photo as in fig.340. The main copy started on the next page.

342. 'Towards the Matt Black Dreamhome', *The Face*, No.67, November 1985
The subject matter here required a layout that emphasised its three-dimensionality, also needing to convey the objects' preciousness and their function's familiarity. The headline type was computer-condensed — a short-lived shift away from hand-drawn type to a facility that supposedly allowed direct control over the shape of letterforms. The block of type overstated the assumed classicism and neutrality suggested by the use of black.

343. Paul Smith, *The Face*, No.63, July 1985
344. Paul Weller, *The Face*, No.62, June 1985
345. 'Trials By Telly', *The Face*, No.62, June 1985

'I think a lot happened on *The Face* because, having no experience of glossy magazines, we haven't felt hidebound by conventions. We've been able to develop. By the same token, it's funny how quickly a magazine develops its own traditions.' (Nick Logan).

The headlines' literal meanings were undermined by using any one of the several typefaces Brody had designed since issue 50 of *The Face*. This was modular design in its true sense, the language of supermarket shelves, marking the end of Brody's reliance on pre-designed type founts.

346. 'Eire's Teenage Auto Rampage', *The Face*, **No.67, November 1985**
The headline achieves documentary emphasis through the simple technique of boxing the operative word. The border around the photograph gives the impression that it has been lifted and dropped into the spread without modifying its format to that of *The Face*.

348. 'Collapsing New Buildings', *The Face*, **No.61, May 1985**
'Architects, painters and sculptors must recognise once more the nature of buildings as composite entities. Only then will their works be permeated with that architectonic feeling which has become lost in the art of the salons'.
(Walter Gropius, quoted in Reyner Banham, *Theory and Design in the First Machine Age*, The Architectural Press, 1960).

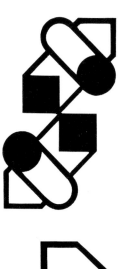

347. Motifs for the main text of 'Collapsing New Buildings'

349. 'The Face Review of 1985', The Face, No. 70, February 1986
Editor Paul Rambali came up with the idea of using a photograph of Madonna to sum up the year in question. Brody cropped the photograph to isolate just enough of Madonna's features for her to remain recognisable. It was at this point (and in fig. 346) that the headlines were being drawn specifically for each feature. The caption was placed in a square block, a system that was followed throughout the rest of the review.

350. 'Latina', The Face, No. 76, August 1986
The problem here was to articulate a feature that comprised two separate pieces of writing. The two introductions start with the same voice before moving into their respective text sections. The use of apparently unrelated blocks of imagery created a sense of the subject matter without being specific, the main illustrative force being carried by the headline.

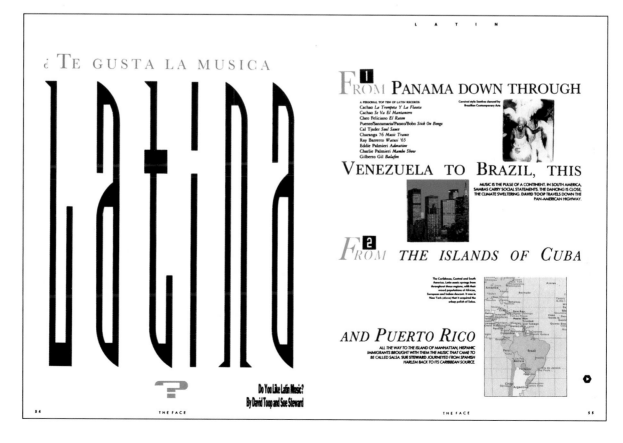

PARIS

Paris

Photography ANDREW MACPHERSON *Texts* PATRICK ZERBIB

THEY ARE COMING TO BE KNOWN AS THE *FAST YEARS:* A SOCIAL EXPERIMENT TO STEER A COUNTRY INTO THE FUTURE...

half a decade of heated expansion and equally heated debate have enriched the arts, technology and communications, but now the creative boom is under threat. A new right-wing force in politics admires the Thatcherism that, ironically, leaves Britain with lower growth and far worse unemployment than France has had under the Socialists: The existence of TV6, an all-music channel, is threatened; just one of numerous openings created by liberal ideals. These have helped Paris to live, at last, its dream of being the great cosmopolitan city. In the streets, the clubs, the galleries and cinemas, different cultures and publics meet. Sidiki Bakaba, a star of the African cinema, says that for him, Paris is a suburb of Africa. Alpha Blondy, Ray Lema and **Kassav**, with music from North Africa and the Caribbean, fill Paris concert halls. Their success here has made them stars at home, but the French media remain deaf to this explosion. Kassav, the third biggest French group in terms of record sales, are never seen on television. In other ways too, Paris is the crossroads of continents and cultures. The music of the third world, the design acumen of Europe, the fashion of Japan, all find a fertile soil here. Meanwhile, cinema and video arts, fashion and painting from Paris are ex-ported around Europe and the US. But there are problems ... The French cinema annually discovers a starlet like **Beatrice Dalle** but because of tight-knit and conservative movie production houses, new directors like Diane Kurys or Coline Serreau have to go to America to find work. The art of video in France has produced some imaginative results, yet Cora can't raise the budget for his next project and Mondino prefers to shoot clips for Madonna in Los Angeles. French fashion designers and entrepreneurs have to go to New York to flourish, like Marie-Paul who called her shop Maripol. Under the influence of Jack Lang, politics and culture were reconciled, but the experiment has now been interrupted by the conservatives ... What next? Paris in the Forties was 'existentialism', when intellectuals like Sartre and committed singers like Juliet Greco took over the Left Bank; Paris in the Sixties was the 'nouvelle vague', when the young rebel movie director Godard and the scandalous act-ress Bardot threatened to set fire to the middle-class; the Seventies was consumed by rock, comics and drugs. Paris in the Eighties is waiting for definition ...

THE FACE · 46 · 47 · THE FACE

FREDERIC ANDREI WAS THE OPERA-LOVING POSTBOY IN JEAN-JACQUES BENEIX'S MOVIE *DIVA*, THE FRENCH FILM THAT HELPED DEFINE THE STYLE OF POP VIDEOS AND MOVIES IN THE EIGHTIES. HE'S JUST COMPLETED *PARIS MINUIT*, WHICH HE DIRECTED AND STARS IN.

ELIZABETH DJIAN IS THE STYLIST WHO GAVE JILL MAGAZINE ITS DISTINCTIVE CHARACTER, LENDING CLASS TO OUTRAGEOUS CLOTHES AND WIT TO CLASSICS. SHE STYLED OUR OPENING FASHION STORY.

ANTOINE DE CAUNES

DIANE KURYS

ALAIN BASHUNG

JACK LANG

AS MINISTER OF CULTURE DURING MITTERAND'S PRESIDENCY, JACK LANG ENVIGORATED THE ARTISTIC LIFE OF THE CAPITAL.

THE FACE

---

357. *Opposite:* **Duran Duran, *The Face*, No.68, December 1985**
358. **'China — The Disco Revolution', *The Face*, No.68, December 1984**
The 'China' spread gave the impression of a single image by using six small ones of equal size.

351/352/253/354/355/366. Paris story, *The Face*, No.74, June 1986
The feature was an attempt to communicate the feeling of a city with its many creative talents and individual lifestyles. The structure was carefully interwoven, with different typefaces for the many captions which accompanied the variously treated photographic portraits. The main headline, again unique to this feature, was given a luxury of space rare in magazine layouts. It needed to be simple and cohesive — often difficult with single word headlines — as a direct balance to the convoluted format of the rest of the feature. The design was playful, following no clear rules except those that were self-determined. The fashion pages were also treated differently — apart from the opening spreads (shown here) where the type was given an unlikely prominence, the remaining pages after fig.366 included only the folio and page number.

'Towards the end of working with *the Face*, I wanted the design to reach a point of maturity. Even experimentation has to be challenged. I was looking at all the designs that I'd come up with and wanted to refine them into a new language.'

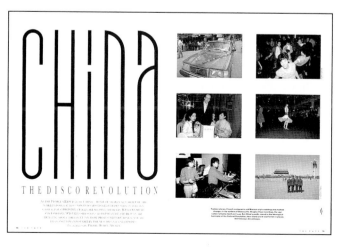

I**N** HIS UNFORGETTABLE PERFORMANCE AS

TRUTH IS LIES THE FEARSOME

PRINT BARON OF P*RAVDA*,

A**NTHONY** H**OPKINS** MAKES LIES SEEM

ALLURING.

A**S A** W**ELSH**

ACTOR ON

THE VERGE

OF MAJOR

STATUS, HE

HAS LEARNED TO STOP

LOOKING FOR TRUTH.

Silence . . .

T**HE** SCENE IS THE sprawling BBC studios in Ealing; the set is dressing room number 103. It is empty except for a sofa and dressing table on which lies open a copy of *King Lear* with lines underlined neatly in red Biro. There is also a Polaroid of a man with cotton-wool hair, a bottle of Eye Dew, a sachet of Sweet and Low and a large pair of teardrop-shaped spectacles.

Enter stage right.

A**NTHONY** H**OPKINS** *(with dignity)* "I'm sorry to keep you waiting."

H**E** IS A SMALLISH, plumpish, middle-ageish figure wearing a shirt whose cornflower-coloured stripes highlight the luminescent blue of wide, kindly eyes. The manner is gentle but direct, a professional interviewee uncomfortable with personal questions — but voluble on the subject of his work. Work is uppermost in his mind nowadays — there's so much of it. Apart from regular voiceovers and helping out with Sports Aid

Anthony Hopkins by Jessica Berens/Photography John Stoddart

THE FACE 31

FUN WITH MONOTONY

Phillip Glass by Sheryl Garratt/Photo Martyn J. Adelman

P**HILLIP** G**LASS**
REPEATS
HIMSELF FOR
THE BENEFIT OF
OF THE P**OPULAR**
AUDIENCE

I AM SITTING IN A chair where Doris Lessing was sitting only hours before, talking to Al Jolson's great-nephew. Some people say that this man is "the most significant composer of our time", so I'm asking him about his composition technique and he's telling me about beaches and Leonardo da Vinci. "Close your eyes now and imagine a painting you've seen — say, the Mona Lisa. Can you see it? Well, that's how I visualise music. Music is always very concrete to me in the same way that you can close your eyes and imagine the place you lived in ten years ago. When you can do that — let's say you imagine a beach that you're on — then imagine you're walking on the beach, then imagine yourself with a dog. Then get rid of the dog and put a bird there, and then get rid of the bird and put a kite there."

G L A S S

36 THE FACE

THE FACE 37

359. Anthony Hopkins, *The Face*, No.75, July 1986
360. Philip Glass, *The Face*, No.75, July 1986

The use of Baskerville Small Caps. as the typeface for the introductory text continued the refinement of Brody's design for *The Face*. Initially, it carried the same weight as the headline, which was given emphasis through a device such as reversing out type from a black bar. The classicism that the design implied together with the precious care with which the photographs were treated announced the end of typographic experimentation and pointed towards a less frantic, calmer approach. This was Brody's penultimate issue as art director of *The Face*, fig.17 being from the last one he designed.

[SQUARE] [BASHING]

THEY PROJECT IMAGES OF FASCISM INSIDE THE RUINS OF INDUSTRIAL BRITAIN. THEN THEY TAKE MORE DEBRIS AND USE IT TO MAKE MUSIC, A THUNDEROUS ALARM FOR A SLEEPING NATION. BY WAVING THE BONES AT THE OLD IDOLS, TEST DEPARTMENT HOPE TO NEGATE THEIR POWER AND DRIVE THEM OFF. TO BANG THE MESSAGE HOME, THEY TOOK THIS VOODOO ON A TOUR OF THE COLLIERIES, FOLLOWED BY ONE OF EASTERN EUROPE. *Text* ROSE ROUSE *Photographs* JEFF VEITCH

TEST DEPARTMENT WERE FORMED during the autumn of 1981. The industrial wasteland of New Cross in South London was their playground. Beating the shit out of scrap metal became their domain. Defiant non-musicians, they thrived on the primitive physicality of their rhythms. Politics came later but Constructivist artwork, slogans like 'Ecstasy Under Duress' and 'Strength Through Motion' were already there. They played around with both Nazi and Bolshevik imagery and aimed to catalyse via the ensuing confusion. Sometimes, they succeeded.

Rare appearances at places like the railway arches at Waterloo and Cannon St Station cemented a reputation for willful avoidance of the rock circuit, requiring a resourceful response to constant lack of finance. It was a strategy they nurtured, though a police raid at their Waterloo performance — where the tools of their trade were confiscated as offensive weapons — smacked of the hand of manager Stevo, a media terrorist in the bud.

During 1983/84, when metal-bashing was briefly hip, they were lumped together with SPK and Einstürzende Neubauten. Nevertheless, Test Department survived.

As metal hit the music press, however, Ashley Goodhall, then A&R man for Phonogram, signed Test Department as representatives of the new thing. Not surprisingly, their relationship — with Stevo at his worst — didn't last long. But it was a productive encounter for Test Department. Not only did they persuade the record company to release two 12-inch records instead of an album for their "Beating The Retreat" project, they also convinced Polygram that they should issue the distinctly uncommercial video *before* the records. A novel tactic, Polygram strove hard to present it as a radical breakthrough to the rest of the industry.

Veering dangerously near to pure pretension in their work at this time — the SM imagery on the video *Program For Progress* confirming an imaginative drought — the miners strike saved Test Department from further embarrassment. At a point when their ambivalence was becoming a burden,

361. Test Department, *The Face*, No.73, May 1986
True to its subject, the bracketing articulated the fact that the headline was just one element in the layout's construction.

362/363. Expo on *Touch Ritual*, *The Face*, No.73, May 1986
The typeface was specially drawn, in this case complementing the section title to suggest unexposed film — a different sense of possibility to the logo shown in fig.317. The treatment of one magazine within another was an extension of this edition of *Touch*, which concentrated upon the transmutation of media rituals.

364/365. Linford Christie, *The Face*, No.75, July 1986
Again using a small, specifically drawn headline, here the actual text formed a shape which added illustrative form to an editorially cramped layout.

EXPO

TIME BANDIT|

NEW SOCIALIST No. 39 JUNE 1986 **90p/$3**

NEW SOCIALIST

EDGE OF DARKNESS
ROSALIE BERTELL ON THE RADIOACTIVE WORLD

366. Cover for *New Socialist*, No. 39, June 1986
On this cover, Brody used a colour negative image of New York to suggest a nuclear holocaust. The Bodoni type contrasts with the over-Modernist logo. The white strip at the head of the page offsets the textural image and gives the magazine a clear news-stand identity.

THE **NEW UNIONISM**
POLITICS OF **BREASTFEEDING**
WOMEN BEWARE MEN
and
Girlie-pop/Kathy Acker/Cabaret/Mafia

NEW SOCIALIST

'It's the American dream of trying to look youthful: the fear of middle age. The whole of the Left is trying to update its image. With CND, they have a core of followers from the 1950s, which they're stuck with. They're preaching to the converted. They need to appeal to a younger mobile readership and to do that they need a language which can be understood. Design provides that language; it is something that is familiar to the type of reader they need to attract.'
(Neville Brody interviewed by Paul Barker for 'The Irresistible Charm of the New Look', *The Sunday Times*, May 1986)

The language of *The Face* had pretty much become the language of the class of readership to which *New Socialist* wanted to appeal. Brody's work with *City Limits* had been identified with party politics – by this time, he was well aware of the extent to which his designs were, in themselves, becoming significations, abetted by the widespread simulation of his work in other magazines, in advertising, in corporate graphics and so on. Instead of pretending that this was not happening, Brody decided to follow through the work he had done with *The Face*, showing that it had a wider application, but trusting that people would realise the difference between the original and its hybrids. Because at times there did seem to be no difference, Brody's decision to work on *New Socialist*, the Labour Party's in-house monthly magazine, was also a means of highlighting the ever-growing importance of Design, and, more crucially, the different areas to which it was being applied.

'It was a challenge to make politics an interesting enough subject for people to want to read about it, but it was also important to avoid being Political with a capital P. As soon as you are pigeon-holed, you stop moving and become a sitting target. I had wanted my design for *The Face* to encourage challenge and argument, but this did not happen, except in isolated instances such as Dick Hebdige's 1985 article 'Squaring up to The Face' for *Ten-8* magazine. So, by working for *New Socialist*, I hoped to become a moving target, and have people actively question what was going on in the media as a whole. Undoubtedly, one of the right wing's major successes as far as its control of television and print media is concerned has been to force people into believing that sensationalism and materialistic values are given facts of life, and people are not encouraged to consider the means by which these reach the screen or page. So much for the irresistible charm of barbed-wire and new technology. Most people, of course, are not duped by *The Sun*, for example, but millions of people buy it, read it, laugh at it and are incensed by it nevertheless. This points to a particularly English disease – a passive disregard that merely consolidates what caused it.

'Until its re-design, *New Socialist* had been a rather heavy tract, laborious to read, communicating political tedium rather than strongly-felt invective. *City Limits* and *Marxism Today* had taken the lead with their design, but because of the closer alignment that *NS* had with Labour, they had to deal with real politics far earlier, showing how it affected people's everyday life.

'There was no point in continuing to appeal only to the party faithfuls – *NS* needed to start competing on the news-stands, so the first priority was to improve the covers. I gave them striping across the top which was neither black nor white, using colour in a very direct and obvious way. The *NS* logo followed through to the contents page, and with other headings like "Front Line", I wanted to create a corporate flow so that the reader could open it at any page and recognise it as *New Socialist*. With the layout, I created a modern feel, but used typefaces like Bodoni to give a classical balance that reflected the magazine's history of theoretical writing. A much greater emphasis was placed

367/368. The design for *New Socialist* needed elements on the page to counterbalance the greyness of text, which took up the greater percentage of the space. The heavy folio and page number block created a solid anchor; its horizontal movement gave the appearance of a page size larger than A4.

369. Contents page, *New Socialist*, No.38, May 1986 The boldness of the contents page was achieved not by the use of multiple images, but through a single powerful photograph and block of type.

370. Cover for *New Socialist*, No.40, Summer 1986
'This was the third and final cover I designed for *New Socialist*. To make the point that politics should become more actual, I put Parker, Lady Penelope's chauffeur in the TV serial *Thunderbirds*, on the cover to illustrate a feature on 'Stately Home Britain'. It was a way of saying that politics should reflect a language that wasn't high-faluting theory all the time. *New Socialist* expressed a desire to deal with more real subject matter. They brought in a whole range of new writers, and started dealing with women's cinema, Frank Bruno and *Miami Vice*; however, my Parker cover did not go down well with the party machine.

Once I had laid the groundwork for the design, I persuaded them to employ Phil Bicker to carry out its monthly production. This was an example of creative interpretation. Phil adapted my initial concept within weeks and pursued his own direction. The re-design was not a specific instruction, but a feeling that reflected the momentum that *New Socialist* was looking for.'

131

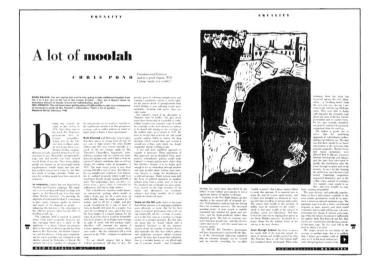

374/375/376. Logos for the corporate identity Brody created for *New Socialist*.

371. 'Feminism and Class Politics', *New Socialist*, No. 38, May 1986
372. 'Reagan's Terrorist Fig Leaf', *New Socialist*, No. 38, May 1986
373. 'A Lot of Moolah', *New Socialist*, No. 38, May 1986

The features were text-based and thus required a clear and structured presentation. Bodoni was used as the main typeface, and by altering its weight, size and letter-spacing, a depth was established to the page that fell within given limits. Images are used illustratively and as graphic symbols, particularly in the top layout.

on the use of photographs, because I felt that the potential new readership had largely brought up on television's fast imagery. The magazine was trying to state its relevance to modern life. The fact that it spoke out against many aspects of this did not mean that it could afford to ignore the prevailing modes of expression.

'Needless to say, the whole exercise triggered a "designer Socialist" backlash. Even though it was what I had suspected might happen, I got fed up with being tagged a left-wing designer. People missed the point that the Left was saying "We want to be modern, we want to be part of your lifestyle." I wanted to show that if politics had become lifestyle, it was surely time to encourage more people to challenge policies. You could apply the same criterion to voting in an election. The choice might be unsatisfactory, but if you choose not to vote, you're seen as being passive. What you've got is all you've got until it changes – and to just sit back and do nothing simply encourages the abolition of voting altogether.'

'If voting changed anything, they'd ban it.'

CITY LIMITS

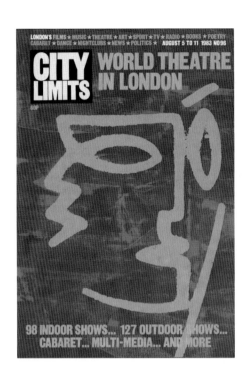

City Limits was started in 1981 as a breakaway magazine from the weekly London guide, *Time Out*, now its major competitor. The latter had grown out of the underground/alternative culture of the late Sixties under owner and one-time editor Tony Elliott. The magazine was set up with a parity pay structure which, by 1980, Elliott felt had become out of key with the staff hierarchy. This was strongly resisted by many of *Time Out*'s writers and contributors; they went on strike.

During this strike, which lasted for months, *Time Out*'s dissenters produced a free listings-sheet, simply called *Not*. Elliott, however, was not about to give in and as a result *City Limits* was formed as a co-operative with the parity pay structure the staff had fought for. *City Limits* wanted to look like a radical magazine in every way; its design brief was given to Dave King, whose use of heavy bars, similar to the work he had done for the Mayakovsky and Rodchenko exhibition catalogues, gave *City Limits* the political identity it was looking for.

'Dave King's design was successful, but only for a short time. He gave the magazine a similar uniform to the one that he'd given Rock Against Racism posters, and it did something you shouldn't do, which is to lay all your cards on the table. People were given the choice "take it or leave it", and there was no possible chance of subversion, no chance of reaching the wider public who might buy *City Limits* because they simply wanted to go out and enjoy themselves. The heavy black bar of the design proved detrimental — it had the effect of a black cloud, and for someone looking for entertainment it looked depressing.

'I worked with *City Limits* from June 1983 to April 1987. My original brief was to come up with a more flexible grid system and a more dynamic structure to the various sections. I had to balance elements that needed to be clearly articulated, with a system that would be interesting week after week, fifty-two issues a year. I was brought in to make the magazine acceptable to a broader public, but it was also a case of financial survival — *City Limits* was in dire straits, with its circulation at only 22,000.

'What I found at *City Limits* was a reluctance and a resistance to change. I realised that the design had to satisfy its core readership as well as attract a wider audience, but there was a fear of re-design which was understandable when you consider the effect design can have on editorial content and the way people respond to it. In the Seventies and early Eighties there was a huge fear of change, and now, suddenly, there's a huge fear of un-change, and people are switching styles without knowing why they're doing it. There's now a mistrust of anything that's been around longer than three weeks!

'I wanted to create something new for the magazine, which they had been trying to do unsuccessfully within Dave King's model, bringing in Letratone tints and angled photos. I built a tight structure so that no matter how bad the printing was, or how little time they had to do the design, the result would still look good. I changed the type from bold condensed to a mixture of Gill and Garamond, which shifted the feel away from newsprint and brought it closer to a magazine style. We got better-quality paper

LONDON'S FILMS ★ MUSIC ★ THEATRE ★ ART ★ SPORT ★ TV ★ RADIO ★ BOOKS ★ POETRY
CABARET ★ DANCE ★ NIGHTCLUBS ★ NEWS ★ POLITICS ★ JANUARY 6 TO 12 NO. 118 60P.

CITY LIMITS

MURDER IN MOSCOW

THE MAKING OF 'GORKI PARK'

PLUS REVOLUTION, MACHISMO AND RELIGION - THE HONORARY CONSUL
ANOREXIA - THE GLAMOROUS KILLER   + FREE FILM TICKETS!

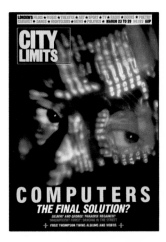

380. *Opposite:* **Cover for** *City Limits*, **No.118, January 1984**
As cover designer, Brody had the opportunity to apply his illustrations to a different outlet. The rough-lined painting for 'Murder in Moscow' was combined with the more graphic symbol of a shooting target. On fig.377 (previous page), Brody used a linear graphic mask to convey a sense of theatre, ensuring tht it would make a visual impact on the news-stand. The line drawing was originally 2 cm in height, and was reproduced out of focus to give the face a soft outline. At this stage, Brody was still using the sans serif typeface introduced by Dave King.

381/382/383. Section openers and contents page for *City Limits*, **1984/1985**
The typographic structure was intentionally flexible; the main priority was the articulation and organisation of the content in a manner that was immediately clear to the reader. The centrally located listings section served as a second cover.

384/385. Covers for *City Limits*, **Nos. 129 and 136, March and May 1984**
The 'Computers' cover was created by projecting an image of a circuit board onto a human face — the human as machinery. The main headlines were now almost always wide-spaced.

386. Listings page in *City Limits*, **No.289, April 1987**
The listings pages had to accommodate a great deal of information whilst retaining visual interest. The system had to be dynamic and easy to use. Section headings were designed to maintain white space, and subsections used white type reversed out of a bar. Large bullets indicated the start of a section. This particular page was from the second re-design.

'With the weekly *City Limits* covers, there was a chance to use different ideas rather than to produce predictable solutions, and because of the magazine's tight budget, these were more often based on an idea rather than an expensive photo-shoot. For example the Dirk Bogarde cover used a four-colour treatment of a black-and-white photograph, and the "Style" cover included Pantone colour swatches saying "DIY Designer Kit". The best-selling issue *City Limits* have so far published was surprisingly the "Sly and Robbie" cover.'

for the cover, moved the features to the front and back, and created a new section in the centre of the magazine as a listings supplement, which, since it had to be run on an inferior paper stock, was printed in dark blue. The original plan was to staple this section separately, so that it could be detached as a more "mobile" guide, and to change the colour of the paper every week on a rotation system, but the budget would not stretch to that. We coined the use of the word "listings", used "Network" for the TV, radio and video section, and brought a racier system to the news stories with "Fast Forwards".

'The new design had its effect on the editorial content as well, and it was said that when the writers realised that people would start to pay more attention to their contributions, there was a minor panic: but they did improve. Suddenly there was space. There were larger photos, a wider page size, and more dynamic covers to give a better news-stand profile. Advertising increased,

and the magazine's sales went up by 50%. The focal point of *City Limits* shifted slightly, at least in the way it was received, and there were deep ideological arguments about the advent of "coverism". It looked less radical. People criticised me for that.

'There was a long period of trying out different column widths for the listings, which above all had to be economical in terms of copy space. Eventually, we came back to the News Gothic that Dave King had used, which for economy and readability at a small size is brilliantly designed; its only problem is an inflexibility at the different weights of bold and normal. Anyway, the design worked well, but *City Limits* had not understood that I had given them a flexible system. They copied the dummy I had designed, and copied it again, and again. That's not what I had wanted. The covers changed, there was a new logo. The result looked a lot more accomplished than *Time Out*, but because of a lack of real art direction due to the magazine's policy of democratic decision-

387. Cover for *City Limits*, No.282, February 1987
The new logo was effective both horizontally and vertically, against the advice of the sales force – *The Face* had once been similarly warned.

388. 'Simply White?', *City Limits*, No.262, October 1986
389. 'An Essential Epic', *City Limits*, No.267, November 1986
The second re-design made a greater use of wide-leaded introductions and type reversed out of blocks. The condensed type could be used larger on the page, improving the depth and rhythm of the magazine.

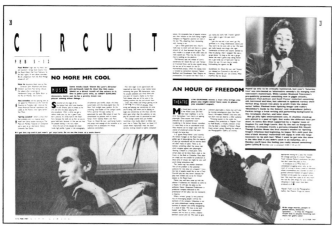

390/391/392. News sections in *City Limits*
The second re-design had to accommodate a more complex editorial structure than its predecessor, with individual sections needing a more sophisticated design to allow for a more compressed and varied content. This economy of space was offset by combining blocks of type with wide-spaced lettering for section titles. The use of condensed Gill brought a greater sense of urgency to the News section. Bars and rules no longer feature as they had done in previous designs for the magazine.

making, the design fell apart within a year because there was nobody to carry it through.

'With any magazine, you cannot come up with one system and expect to maintain it for five years; it needs creative interpretation. When the only way you know how to do this is to bring in something completely different, then inevitably the design will collapse from the centre, which is what happened. This led to the second re-design, which, I must admit, collapsed inward even faster than the first one. *City Limits* had by this time got in-house typesetting facilities with new technology that allowed you to condense and expand — my job was to limit the choices they had for its use. I kept the basic structure pretty much the same, because it had to serve the same function. On the second re-design, the bars that were left became rules; these were placed underneath photos and blocks of information to add an order and a

dynamism to an otherwise grey page. The bullets remained because there seemed to be no point in making them squares. In the "Listings" section, I had a sideways heading that allowed you to flick through the magazine and find the area you wanted to refer to. Also at the front of the listings section I maintained a short contents list so that readers wouldn't have to go back to the head of the magazine every time they wanted to find out information from a different category. Here, signposting becomes even more important than usual.

'After the second re-design, the covers were never better. There was far more range between a completely typographic cover, a graphic one, or a full-colour photo. Inside, I wanted to create a rhythm and a sense of depth. There was an articulated difference between what was feature material, news material and listings. Hopefully, the design also showed that you can be just as radical without shouting it from every page.'

393/394/395/396. Covers for *City Limits*, Nos.263, 266, 275 and 274, October and November 1986 and January 1987
The cover designs return to almost pure typography for the first time since Dave King's departure.

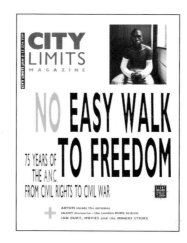

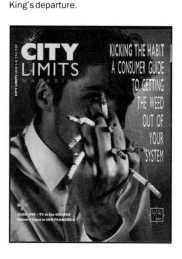

397. No.89,
June 1983

398. No.92,
July 1983
Jamie Morgan

399. No.164,
November 1984

400. No.175,
February 1985
Amanda Searle

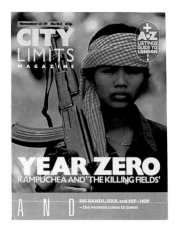

401. No.94,
July 1983
David Corio

402. No.98,
August 1983

403. No.198,
July 1985

404. No.210,
October 1985
Amanda Searle

405. No.97,
August 1983

406. No.102,
September 1983

407. No.214,
November 1985
Sheila Rock

408. No.215,
November 1985

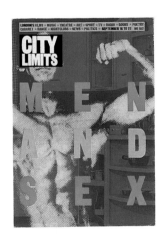
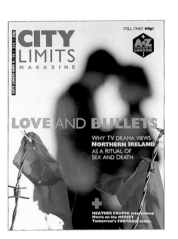
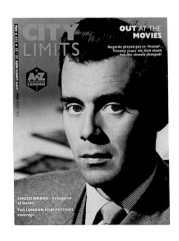

409. No.121,
January 1984

410. No.126,
March 1984
Sheila Rock

411. No.219,
December 1985
Cindy Palmano

412. No.222,
January 1986
Amanda Searle

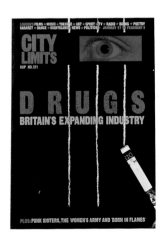
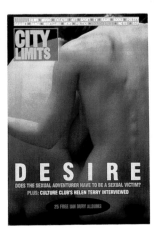
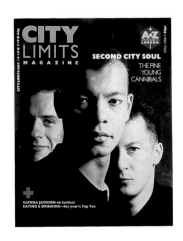

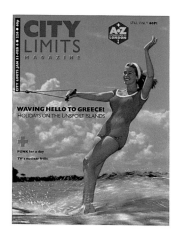

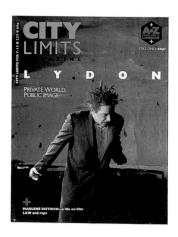

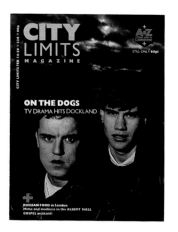

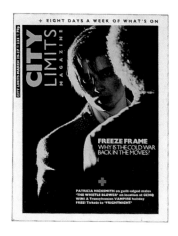

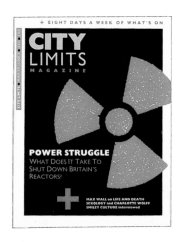

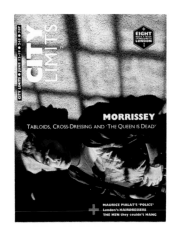

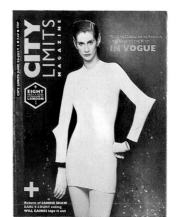

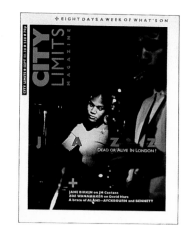

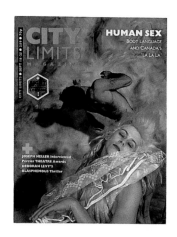

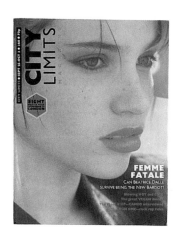

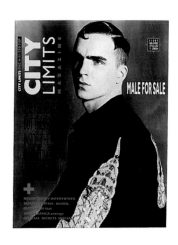

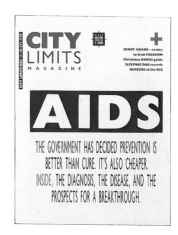

413 No.226,
January 1986

414. No.227,
February 1986
A. J. Barratt

415. No.228,
February 1986
Cindy Palmano

416. No.233,
March 1986
Josef Koudelka

417. No.236,
April 1986
John Butler

418. No.243,
May 1986

419. No.245,
June 1986
Lawrence Watson

420. No.247,
June 1986
Cindy Palmano

421. No.256,
August 1986
John Stoddart

422. No.258,
September 1986
Andrew Macpherson

423. No.259,
September 1986
Edoard Lock

424. No.260,
September 1986

425. No.267,
November 1986
Nick Knight

426. No.268,
November 1986
Neville Brody

427. No.270,
December 1986
Cindy Palmano

428. No.271,
December 1986

ARENA

Arena was launched in 1986 by the publishers of *The Face*, and is edited by Nick Logan. Essentially, it was to be a magazine for readers who had grown out of *The Face*, and also a publication that could have an appeal as a men's magazine, of which there are none on the market in England. *Cosmopolitan* had tried and failed with *Cosmo Man*, and *Unique* is more of a fashion trade publication.

Against all the market research advice that larger publishing companies such as IPC and Condé Nast had come up with for themselves, Nick Logan decided that it was a good direction to take. Its circulation figures have yet to be audited, but the magazine seems to be doing well — worldwide sales are estimated at around 70,000.

'Graphically, the first two issues were still very much in the mould of *The Face*, a heritage that I still hadn't shaken off completely. After getting to grips with the way editorial content was coming together, rather than creating a design that could easily become "the new thing", I thought it was time to stop, to take stock, and to see how the land lay. I wanted to suggest that some of the hysteria should be taken out of contemporary design by adopting a very straightforward, informational approach, using Helvetica for headlines, but still applying it to a system that would allow for a dynamic use of type. I hand-drew a typeface that was used for section headings to carry the identity of the magazine.

'The personality of the magazine is carried more by its structure than the typography or any other individual feature. Most of the sections — "Vanity", "People", "Spectator" etc. — are ironically named after other magazine titles. The design itself was never intended to have a strong identity. I wanted the words and images to dictate the design. It had to be clean, with an elegant use of white space to articulate confidence. It had to be "good quality". A great emphasis is placed on the actual art direction, which dictates the design and not vice-versa; more so than *The Face*, the photographic quality is paramount. *Arena* is also much more consumer-orientated. I do suspect that just as many women as men are buying it; whatever, my design has never been deliberately geared to a male sensibility.

'I did not believe that people would discover things in the design worth ripping off, but they have. What else can be said about *Arena*? It really should speak for itself.'

429. Joe Orton, *Arena*, No.1, Winter 1986
430. 'The X Factor', *Arena*, No.2, Spring 1987
From the outset, a typographic system was established for *Arena* where few elements line up with anything else, unlike the more precise typographic coding that had been a feature of Brody's latter designs for *The Face*. For the main texts, a double-column grid was used with a wide space between the copy. Initially, Brody chose lower-case Garamond Light Condensed for the headlines and text-openers, Helvetica Ultra Compressed for all credits and Kabel Bold for captions and cover lines. The pages thus achieved a subtle contrast through these different weights, and an unsettling rhythm that came from their apparent normality.

431. Cover for *Arena*, No.1, Winter 1986
432. Cover for *Arena*, No.2, Spring 1987
The new hand-drawn logo for *Arena* was intentionally European in feel, extending certain elements of the letterforms in order to be immediately recognisable — somewhat ironically, this device was suggested by an IBM golf-ball typewriter face. The square form of the logo was deliberately Modern, but it also needed to offset the long list of cover lines.

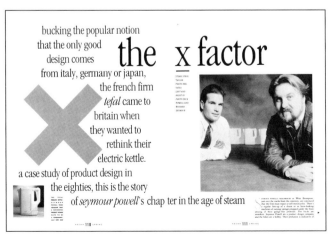

C A S H M E R E

THE ROUGH WITH THE SMOOTH. BRITISH CASH-MERE AND AMERICAN JEANS. *Styling RAY PETRI. Photography MARK LEBON.*

Black cashmere crewneck by Ballantyne at Harrods, London SW1; platinum Porsche watch from Harvey Nichols, London SW1; secondhand Levis from American Classics, 20 Endell St, London WC2, and 404 Kings Rd, London SW10. Model Zane at Beatrice (Milan) and Models 1 (London).

ARENA **44** WINTER

433/434. 'Cashmere' story, *Arena*, No. 1, Winter 1986
The spread clearly shows Brody's use of type to create shapes on the page without resorting to graphic devices – the choice of typeface, however, was soon discarded in favour of a more anonymous format. The folios and page numbers were used to emphasise a centring and to indicate the pages' more static and secure subject matter.

435. Cover for *Arena*, **No.3, Spring/ Summer 1987**
436. 'Dateline Milan', *Arena*, **No.3, Spring/ Summer 1987**
437. Bruce McLean, *Arena*, **No.3, Spring/ Summer 1987**

Helvetica replaced Garamond as the main headline and introduction typeface. Its blandness was further enhanced by using it in purely lower-case form, re-emphasising the informational quality of the design. Photographs were almost always used full bleed, shifting the focus away from the design to the actual image, questioning further the distinction between surface and content.

dateline : milan
in the heat of the night: milan, autumn/winter '87, photographed by norman watson, fashion and text by ray petri,
shot at super studio, milan

striking a pose

sculptor, painter, performance artist,
bruce mclean has been asking
questions about our behaviour for
over twenty years. now he turns his
attention to the living room. *tom
baker* shares a joke with britain's
unsung international art hero

story TOM BAKER *photography* ALISTAIR THAIN

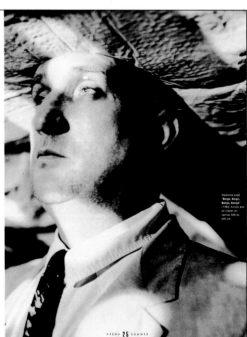

438. Cover for *Arena*, No.4, Summer 1987
439. Jean-Paul Gaultier, *Arena*, No.4, Summer 1987
440. 'Navy and White', *Arena*, No.4, Summer 1987

The informational base to the design was then subverted by using type and image in a modular frame, allowing headlines to be run vertically and white space to dominate certain spreads. Type was pushed into corners or suspended from an arbitrary line. A bold script typeface was used for credit line descriptions.

gaultier

joker in the pack: jean-paul gaultier is the anglophile frenchman with radical designs on men. at 35 he's outgrown the tag *enfant terrible* but not his appetite for outrage

story SARAH MOWER *photography* ANDREW MACPHERSON

navy and white

the summer's dominant colour combination styled by *marcus von ackermann* photographed by *robert erdmann*

'Neville's great strength is to see an idea all the way through, down to the last detail. It's most obvious with *Arena*, where he has virtually designed every page. The magazine is roughly a quarterly, so there is more time to draw all the elements together. Being a monthly, sections of *The Face* were lagging behind the features — sections like "Intro", "Monitor", the letters page and back issues page were all things that Neville had developed the initial ideas for, and then I'd done the design or layout of them and they weren't quite as good' (Nick Logan).

441. 'Spectator' section, *Arena*, No.2, Spring 1987
'Spectator', sited at the front of the magazine, carries both critical review and overview. The section uses the same typeface for its headline as the front cover logo, and the indentation of quotes set in Kabel brings further movement to the pages. The reversed out 'A' together with the solid bar beneath the headline is a parallel to the corporate 'flag' on the cover of *The Face*.

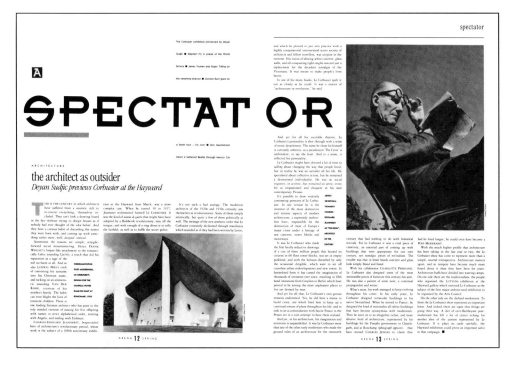

442/443. 'Vanity' and 'People' sections, *Arena*
'Vanity', 'People' and 'Avanti' (see fig. 125) required strong condensed headlines to introduce their respective sections, for which Brody decided to use a typeface that had been drawn-up for certain features in earlier issues. In 'Vanity', ironic use is made of antiquated line illustrations adapted from typographic handbooks.

444. Dieter Rams, *Arena* **No.5, Autumn 1987**
Content dictates the form: this page is an advert.

445/446. 'NYC' story, *Arena*, **No.5, Autumn 1987**
Certain headlines heralded a bolder use of Helvetica, in this case in capitals. The tight spacing where the 'N' overlaps with the 'Y' pinpoints the imposed drawbacks of computer and photo-typesetting. Certain ideas need to be consistently re-stated.

2.
boys from the bronx

fashion by **ray petri** photography **norman watson**
hair by **rayman camacho** (elizabeth watson, NYC)
models **simon de montford** (bethann mgmt), **solo** (Ice), **justin lazard** (click), **david moore** (click), **john enos** (elite)

NYC

1.
urban cowboy: shot on location in new york. fashion by *ray petri* photography *norman watson*

NYC

145

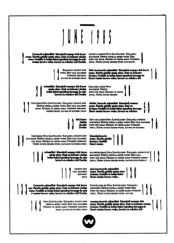

VIVE

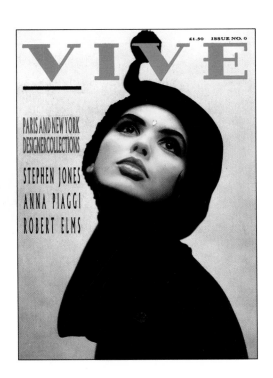

447. Cover for *Vive*, dummy issue, June 1985
The hand-drawn logo for *Vive*, recalls a 1940s magazine in its simplicity.

Vive was a magazine project commissioned by IPC Magazines in 1985. It was going to be a pure fashion magazine — fashion news, fashion features and fashion interviews — an attractive proposition because it would enable me as designer to apply the things I'd learnt with *The Face* to an area that was so obviously concerned with appearance. It could provide a pure challenge — instead of using design to contrast with and to question existing styles, here was a chance to create something that was more open. With all the other work that I've done in this medium, it's usually been a case of adapting existing models. *Vive* did not need to be governed by precedents.

'Unfortunately, the project never got as far as publication. Although IPC were delighted with the dummy, for financial reasons best known to themselves, the company was only prepared to back it for one issue and then "see how it went". Having put so much work into the dummy — and into typographic ideas that I had worked through with Phil Bicker — I didn't then want to put it all on a plate for other people to rip off if the magazine wasn't going to continue beyond the first issue. In many ways, it was ahead of its time.

'I had some bad experiences with other magazine publishers around this time. I was commissioned by *Mademoiselle*, which had the benefit of an art department whose staff would probably outnumber the entire workforce of a British fashion magazine.

'Alexander Libermann, who oversees the Condé Nast group's worldwide art direction, told me, when I suggested designing a typeface for *Mademoiselle*, that "magazines are there to be read one day and binned the next". He thought my final designs were too bold, even though he had seen the preliminary ideas, and felt that something more feminine and "pastel" was required. This did not strike me as what most women would want, but he did not think my design was passive enough. I left them to get on with it.'

448. *Opposite:* **Contents page for** *Vive*, **dummy issue, June 1985**
The contents page combined condensed Albertus type with descriptive copy whose line depth was standardised to create a dynamic flow of information.

449. '**Paris/New York**', *Vive*, **dummy issue, June 1985**
Each fashion story was announced with a right-hand page of type, forming an unmistakable structure and clearly separating editorial from advertising.

450. **Anna Piaggi,** *Vive*, **dummy issue, June 1985**
Quotes were indented into the main copy in a script typeface. Headlines were wide-spaced Weiss initials, with Baskerville capitals being used for the straplines. Corvinus was used for the centred subtitles, with thin rules minimally used for emphasis. The credits were set in a combination of Eurostyle and Bodoni.

451. **Subscriptions page,** *Vive*, **dummy issue, June 1985**
Certain pages were reversed out of black to create surprises.

DESIGNER IN FOCUS

KEEPING UP WITH THE JONES

A QUESTION OF STYLE

STEPHEN JONES IS THE MAKER OF THE MOST STYLISH HATS IN THE WORLD

452. **Stephen Jones,** *Vive*, **dummy issue, June 1985**
Copy openings invariably differed in shape, replacing the need for a bullet or a dropped capital. The caption, photo and text slot playfully together as if in a building or a town-plan.

453. **Masthead page,** *Vive*, **dummy issue, June 1985**
The masthead — as the list of a magazine's backers, staff and contributors is known — was pivoted by a circular logo, with a vertical treatment of the dateline. An enlarged photograph highlighted the subject matter of *Vive*.

POSTERS

There are no general rules that can easily be applied to poster design. Some might say that a poster's information should be visible from a great distance, usually people from advertising agencies and record companies. In the latter case, entire cover designs are simplified down to no more than a single line of type or a single face. Since such posters often have to compete alongside many others on the same site, their content is reduced to such basic levels of information that any distinctiveness is difficult to achieve, with the result that they all tend to shout at the same volume. When information is not trying to say anything, but simply trying to sell something, the fragmented areas of different consumer targets are held together by repetition, not only out of their volume of coverage: advertising language has a limited vocabulary.

'Anything is arguable and you should mistrust any claim that "this is how a poster should look". Depending on specific usage, you could say that a poster exists only to attract attention to the type on it, no matter what the image, or conversely, that a poster should primarily be attractive and the information it carries of secondary importance. People like to keep or buy posters to put up on their walls.

'Take the Photographers' Gallery posters, for example. Since their content obviously comes from a photographic base, you have to treat the given image with respect and use a typeface that not only complements the photograph, but allows it to sit as the most crucial element of the design, at the same time as giving the Photographers' Gallery a consistent identity. The gallery's posters serve a dual purpose — on the reverse of the main design is a more textual breakdown of all the current activities in the gallery; 3,000 are folded from A2 to A4 size and sent out as newsletters, so they must also work by encouraging people to open them out and read the information they carry. But there again, they do have to work on pinboards, in schools, colleges and other institutions. Thirdly, they must work as desirable objects. Since they are posters to promote a non-commercial gallery, I try to bring a confidence and a sense of elegance to them that avoids the "hard sell" approach.

'The posters for the Museum of Modern Art in Oxford require a similar treatment, even though they don't need to double as news-sheets. With "Observers of Man", for example, I followed my reaction to the whole exhibition which showed original photographs taken by early explorers. I wanted to find a way, within modern technology, of expressing this colonised primitivism alongside the development of photographic techniques that can be seen in the work of early explorers. I wanted to express this primitivism rather than illustrate it.

'I find the concept of doing posters for galleries challenging because, in a sense, it's a question of ethics. Do you allow the design to communicate anything in itself, apart from the actual work? This is of course unavoidable, so rather than being ignorant about it, you make it a positive force for people to realise the two sides of what is being communicated — the design and its subject. Whatever the medium of communication, be it spoken word or visual image, you make a decision to apply what you want to communicate in the most pertinent form. It can be seen as an involvement and as a kind of translation — unless, that is, you are merely regurgitating the material supplied, which in some situations is all a designer can do, in spite of any ideas you might have.'

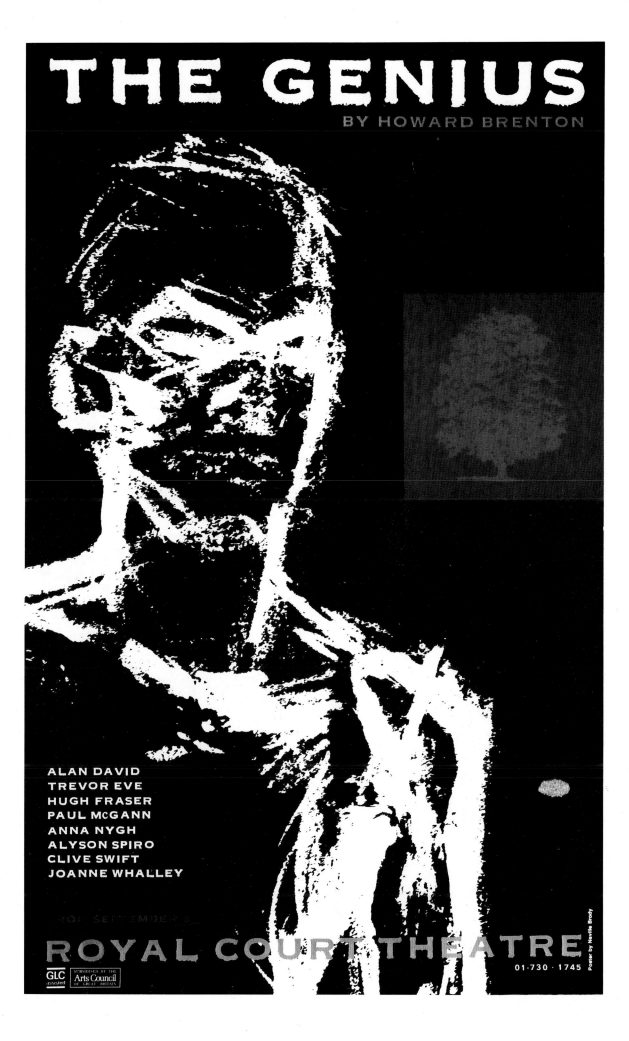

454. *Opposite:* **Poster for the Arthur Tress exhibition,** *Talisman*, **the Museum of Modern Art, Oxford, 1987**

455. *Observers of Man*, **the Museum of Modern Art, Oxford, 1983**

456. *The Genius*, **by Howard Brenton, Royal Court Theatre, 1983**
'There was no given image for *The Genius*, so one had to be created for it. I chose to use a life-drawing—a form that I had been studying in the evening at St Martin's School of Art; also a good form of relaxation. The play was about man against nature. Unfortunately, the colour mark-up was not strictly followed by the printers—this is the sort of thing that happens when working on a low budget.'

457. *Hitting Town*, by Stephen Poliakoff, Oxford University Players, Oriel and ETC, 1983
'Written by Poliakoff, *Hitting Town* was a college play. Its theme was inner-city madness, that sense of being walled in by your own environment. I crossed the idea of urban decay with a primitivism that suggested confused identities. The result had to be equally effective both as a poster and as an A5 hand-out.'

458. *The Pope's Wedding/Saved*, **by Edward Bond, Royal Court Theatre, 1984**
'The Pope's Wedding and Saved were impossible to illustrate together; these two plays were running concurrently in repertory, so I chose a related graphic treatment where the type was very 'distressed'. They were printed in two colours, red and blue, reversing them accordingly so that 50% were run on a red background and 50% on blue. The idea with the graphic technique was to have the two posters alongside each other so that you read them as one: *The Pope's Wedding Saved*.'

459. *Panic*, **by Alan Brown, Royal Court Theatre, 1984**
'I tried to emphasise *Panic* by expressing the opposite. It is a very quiet poster — I wanted to build a tension by placing the word 'Panic' at the bottom, whereas by rights it should be at the top or in the middle. I wanted to express a suppressed energy that makes you feel like screaming.'

460/461. Film posters, *Taboo*, **1981**

PHOTOGRAPHY AS **PERFORMANCE**

[MESSAGE THROUGH OBJECT AND PICTURE **12 SEPTEMBER – 18 OCTOBER**

[INSTALLATION BY JOHN HARPER
12 SEPTEMBER – 11 OCTOBER   **FROM TIME TO TIME**

THE PHOTOGRAPHERS' GALLERY

5 + 8 GREAT NEWPORT STREET, LONDON WC2. TUESDAY TO SATURDAY 11-7

462. *Opposite:*
***Photography as
Performance***, The
Photographers' Gallery,
September/October 1986

463. *Image and
Exploration*, The
Photographers' Gallery,
June/August 1985

464. *Sam Wagstaff/
Eamonn McCabe*, The
Photographers' Gallery,
November 1985/
January 1986

465. *The Animal in
Photography*, The
Photographers' Gallery,
June/September 1986

466. *David Goldblatt/
South Africa*, The
Photographers' Gallery,
April/May 1986

467/468/469/470. Inserts for *Touch Meridians 2*, Touch 1983
Released in two parts, the second *Touch* magazine included a set of 32 prints that corresponded to different pieces of music on a 60 minute cassette. The theme was to produce a better connection towards a shared aim, that of creating a medium that appeals to *all* the senses. The composition was based on the meridian points of the human body or on maps, which represented some of the perennial drawbacks of 'independent' initiatives in the media — experimentation that works in isolation from the mainstream to which it is directed; 'specialisation' becomes another satellite state amidst a host of social and cultural categories: a means of separation. In collaboration with Chris Moretone, Brody developed this idea and, using PMT overlays, processed one image that was then divided into North, South, East and West. The four worked individually, but were coded by a series of thin white rules that matched up to create an abstract poster. Whether this arrangement was made or not was a further extension of the magazine's theme — to encourage active participation.

471. Cover poster for _Touch Travel_, Touch 1984

Brody worked with designer Garry Mouat on the third _Touch_. Mouat decided to complement the edition's theme by presenting the magazine as four A2-sized posters that folded to A5 – like Ordnance Survey maps or a city-guide. The texts on each poster were overlaid upon images and objects handed to _Touch_ for the project, each one expressing a different aspect of travel: a Kabuki mask from Japan, a bird's feather from Nepal, a photo of the first lunar footsteps made by Armstrong in 1969, and shown here (the right way up), a Madonna's face. Brody and Mouat abstracted these on the PMT camera, bringing in additional travel elements. Again, different texts and images related to a 60 minute cassette that, amongst other sources, included music from Bali, Eire and Venezuela.

'What we know, or think we know about other cultures, is strained through a muslin of myth, maybe elaborated by the armchair tourism of such programmes as "Daktari" and even "The World About Us": a stock of predominantly visual impressions, like a vast collection of postcards, most of them cosmetic and manipulated.

Tourists want to see ritual, and for the sake of their cash, rich layers of tradition and art are sliced through, so that the foreigner can swallow a chunk of exoticism without too much effort. The terms of this recreation may be firmly set, because so long as tourists have even a small degree of their fantasies of primitivism confirmed, the native expectation of foreigners is correspondingly fulfilled. We think we are just looking, but really we are worked deep into the performance.'
(Clare Wilkinson, in _Touch Travel_, Touch 1984).

[LANGUAGE]

'Many abbreviations are so seldom expanded that their precise significations are forgotten. T.B. stands for Tubercle Bacillus: G.I. for General Issue. Abbreviations are not always time-savers: they may become linguistic pests. Like slang, abbreviations may be of short life. They are shadowy and inhuman devices appearing and disappearing in that strange border country which separates speech from the mathematical sciences.'
(Simeon Potter, *Our Language*, Penguin Books, 1950)

I n his book, *Our Language*, Potter relates the 'odd coincidence' that the initial names of King Charles II's ministers, Clifford, Arlington, Buckingham, Ashley, and Lauderdale, form the word 'cabal', akin to the ancient Hebrew 'cabbala', suggesting a secret 'clique or faction'. Potter also refers to a long list of acronyms and abbreviations of which only UNESCO, FIAT and LSO still mean anything; others such as SCAPA, the Society for Checking the Abuses of Public Advertising, have since disappeared. Today, think of the power of signification embodied in the initials BBC, CBS, CIA, IRA, USA etc. — their use becomes more assertive as a means of saving time, both for headline writers and their compliant readers. Words become visual slogans. Political abbreviations, especially those ascribed to terrorist organisations/freedom fighters (delete as applicable), help to keep their ideologies at a distance. In 1986, Prime Minister Thatcher referred to the need to further control their 'oxygen of publicity' — just as many have suffered after too stifling an exposure to it.

The number of pop groups and record labels whose names are made up of initials is enormous; now, magazines called *Q* and *W* add to this plethora. What are we meant to deduce from these latter titles? Nothing. This is designer silence, the last refuge of a market-place where ideas are smothered at birth: where styles move so fast that ideas are not given any incubation period before being commercially highlighted and abbreviated.

The above are obvious examples with which to illustrate a trait of human nature — that of finding the quickest though not necessarily the best means of establishing and then proceeding from A to B. There is, for instance, a great distance between what AIDS stands for, and the way its abbreviation-as-slogan has been used like a black talisman in the media to project fear, and to vilify any way of life that falls outside a very cloistered definition of 'normality'.

However, any challenge to the media's control of our perceptions is carefully coded. It is a process wherein challenge itself becomes specialisation, with criticism so diversified that it loses its power and becomes yet another convention — institutions such as Nuclear Power, Unemployment, Third World Exploitation, Racism, Sexism, Drugs, Royalty, Cruelty to Animals, Environmental Abuse, Violence (especially mass murder and sex crimes) and now AIDS. All can be abbreviated to recognisable symbols: the mushroom cloud, the dole queue (and its mythical figure of 3 million), the police photofit, a smoking beagle, etc. Here, the obvious and directly expressed as a challenge can then be easily absorbed.

The drugs problem and AIDS are visually symbolised by a needle dripping blood, but what created AIDS or today's heroin problem? Don't ask. Awkward questions can be readily dismissed as 'lunacy' for daring to fall outside these strict parameters. In this way, as with other forms of cultural expression, *the means* becomes the content. All that remains are 'dissidents', 'subversives', and photographs of rioters taken from behind police lines. Everything is framed.

Language is about the fixing of boundaries and the establishment of systems, but once political, social and economic frameworks have been set up, they assume their own autonomous expression whose uncovering can often be simple (try reading the opposite into any political speech, or interchanging pronouns in any text). Again, 'specialist' language extends into areas which encourage their expressions to be taken for granted, with calamitous results: TV news, for example. It is the difference between the uniform itself and the many reasons for wearing one.

In the media, the coverage of AIDS acts as a suitable metaphor for concentrating ideology. This is now a visual phenomenon, expressed through design. However, here there are no craftsmen, only 'consultants'. A national campaign was mounted by the British government in 1987 to warn people of the dangers of AIDS, deploying, on the one hand, leaflets to every household that fell through the letterbox alongside 'money off' new product coupons and estate agents' circulars; outside, prime-site billboards were booked, their posters using gravestone imagery and a condensed typeface very much in the style of a doomy rock band's LP cover. Evidently, the posters had to appeal to the age group that buys and listens to pop records; would not a billboard that looked like a Michael Jackson sleeve have been more appropriate, then? Alas, no; Pepsi-Cola had got there first, for Michael Jackson is an abbreviation of a greater set of ideologies — consumerism, youth, power and pop music — whose boundaries, once delineated, need a focal point.

In Africa, AIDS is known as 'Slim', referring to the wasting effect of the disease upon the human form. Any attempt to reform the damage will need more than a vaccine.

'Television, the most subtle and powerful source of information, education and ideology in history, is here today, gone tomorrow. Television is the medium that leaves behind no written record, no visible artefacts, no historical trace, no publicly available memory.

The Media Rule: Those who control the present control the past. Those who control the past control the future.'
(Anthony Wilden, *The Rules Are No Game*, Routledge & Kegan Paul, 1987)

Television permeates every aspect of life. It is a means of organising reality, and it abbreviates everything — a result, if nothing else, of the size of its screen. However, it would be misleading to highlight television as a major cause of so many linguistic and historical abbreviations without addressing ourselves to the reasons for this proxy — namely, that many people have been quite happy to be lazy. Their assumed lack of power as passive viewers has become more entrenched, but not because television is, in itself powerful. Its control would become self-evident if nobody watched it. Television and the advertising revenues that support it are above all dependent on a confidence

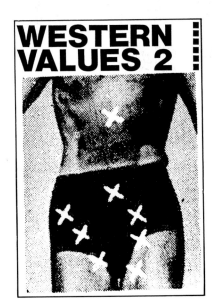

472. *Western Values*, college fanzine, 1978

473. 'The Death of Typography', *Touch Ritual*, Touch, 1986

trick, which grows in strength the longer it goes unchallenged. This much is clear whenever the time comes for a General Election.

How this applies to the AIDS example can be seen in a number of ways, notably as a violent example of the media's shamanistic role, far from being a healing force. Just as significant is the notion of eliminating risk, which permeates deep into the common language. When the most widespread use of language is one that speaks to an imagined lowest common denominator, its subjects become caught in a spiral of receding expression, to deviate from which is to risk being misunderstood. Visual language thereby becomes 'universal'; it is assumed that dictionaries are no longer referred to. This can also work the other way — when advertisers seek to capture a specialist market, they deceive through flattery, often using the language of Art (and Surrealism in particular) to appeal to jaded senses.

Any form of communication, and we have shown that this particularly applies to design, has become a question not of quality, not of empathy, most definitely not of accurate communication, but of speed. The best artwork arrives before the deadline. There are schedules to meet — not that it should be any other way — simply that there are more and more of them, moving at such regularity that the hope of comprehending anything more than any work's instantaneous effect is wishful thinking, and the result

'Ancient art was not for liking. Everyone who read understood. Now, the purpose of art is entirely forgotten.

For instance, take architecture. I saw some examples of architecture in Persia and Turkey — for instance, one building of two rooms. Everyone who entered these rooms, whether young or old, whether English or Persian, wept. This happened with people of different backgrounds and education. We continued this experiment for two or three weeks and observed everybody's reactions. The result was always the same. We especially chose cheerful people.'
(Gurdjieff, 'Questions and Answers on Art Etc.', 1924, in *Views From The Real World*, Arkana *Books, 1984*)

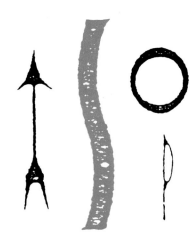

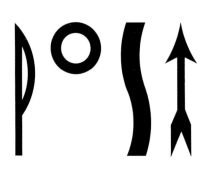

474. Logo for Post, furniture design partnership, 1987

is confusion. How is the public meant to fathom meanings which were never present in the first place? If the main motive is financial and celebrity-seeking, there is *very little* to say about the content. Upon being challenged to make observations on their work, how often do performers, designers and their agents relate some variation of the self-referential 'in-joke'? This process also explains why 'taste' and various forms of style-watching have become such elevated virtues. The commercial world is governed by the economic standpoint that 'trends' are more important than actuality, what might be about to happen more important than what is already there. The season's new colours are rotated and selected as if by a roulette wheel. The confidence trick maintained by the media is no different from that which controls the Stock Exchange and the gambling house. No time is allowed for contemplation, and coupled with television's use of fast editing and micro-narratives, memory becomes increasingly overloaded, and declining attention spans continue to decline.

Words such as 'signification' and 'intensification' illustrate another side of the language problem we presently face. Language is cut and spliced. The suffix '-ation' of today's everyday expression ('hospitalisation', 'falsification') indicates a process where the word becomes longer but its meanings disconnected or, at best, compressed. To many, 'non-violence' might be a roundabout way of saying 'peace', but such has the latter word been abused in the media's counterblast against the 'peace movement', and more recently against the 'peace convoy', that an alternative expression becomes a necessity. 'Peace' is no longer read for its full meaning, but recognised as a 'stance' or a 'policy'. Writing about his experiences in Vietnam, John Pilger relates a more vivid disembowelment of the word:

' "Pacification" was a term which became familiar to many newspaper readers and television viewers but was seldom understood. "Pacification", like "collateral damage", was part of the distortion of language employed to preserve the war's facade. It meant killing as many people as possible in a given area within a given period of time.'
(John Pilger, *Heroes*, Jonathan Cape, 1986)

How do you abbreviate a war visually? For many, Vietnam was represented by the direct symbol of a photograph showing a child burned by Napalm; just as crucial is the process through which visual information is treated and transmitted. One of the most disturbing features of the Vietnam War for the American public, left at home, was that its footage was in colour for the first time, and disturbing 'action scenes' were presented to them without the familiar Hollywood triumph.

Intensity goes hand in hand with simplification to achieve the necessary show of strength for the chosen focus. Stars such as Michael Jackson become 'bigger' and 'bigger' not because they earned their status out of the pure emancipatory and liberating quality of their work. Quite the opposite. When an artist's work is canonised by the media, it is both a means of confirming the latter's own power and an effective absorption of any (challenging) content. The language of fashion goes a lot further than its promise of personal transformation suggests, but it is never more than a skin graft. Today, one speaks of 'power breakfasts' in the City as an important factor in securing deals. The effectiveness of language is increasingly dependent upon the aggressive degree of force with which it is applied. If words and symbols can be misused to the point of their meaning's extinction, does it not follow that a similar fate might await mankind?

Think of 'Live Aid' and 'USA For Africa', famine relief projects that were organised through, by and large, the efforts of a few dedicated individuals. They were successful in realising the immediate objective of raising a large amount of money, but to do this, both concerts were more of a celebration of the power of the Western music business than they were to do with Africa. Everything could be reduced down to the visual representation of an

outline of Africa below a guitar neck. When a situation arose that demanded the most money in the shortest possible time there was, however, no question of including 'ethnic' groups to directly relate their own experience.

'Before, you had to leave in order to arrive. Now things arrive before anyone's leaving. We can wonder what we will wait for when we no longer need to wait in order to arrive. The answer: we will wait for the coming of what remains. These sentences seem paradoxical, but they aren't: the end of departures, generalised arrivals . . . That's what the passengers of the empty circle are trying out, what they're already outlining by hurrying to go nowhere. Of course they still leave and come back for the moment, but they're waiting to be able to arrive without leaving.'
(Virilio/Lotringer, *Pure War*, Semiotext(e), 1983)

This is the updating of Robert Louis Stevenson's maxim that 'to travel hopefully is a better thing than to arrive', except now we are on a conveyor belt. This is not travel, but tourism, where there is no such thing as movement. Such travel is a carefully coded 'activity', yet nobody moves much when they're on a plane. The same desecration that turns a village, a stretch of coastline or a news item into a 'resort', just another stop-over in the global village, is also affecting every language. World travel confirms the idea of process, but the fact that the Western version is as hidden as the different cultural processes with which it comes into contact makes any travel experience a superficial one. For the silent majority, once again it is no longer a question of safeguarding the differences between cultural and linguistic expressions, but of merging them into 'universal language'. However, this is the most colourless of communications. The distinctions of race: an insidious racism. Once everything has become commercially coded, only then is the observer free to move between two points — like switching channels on TV — and once A and B have been fixed as focal points, only then can they be visited. So much for freedom of choice, the construct upon which Western Civilisation is based.

The post-colonialism of air travel and pop music, national flags and Coca-Cola can be made miniature, and its armies invisible — or, at least, no larger those on Japanese pocket-computer games. There is, of course, no chance of winning on such a circuit — a vivid example of information as loop system.

Where there is no differentiation and no contrast, everything is reduced to the level of unimportance. Nothing can be relative when everything is the same, and the codes that govern choice become increasingly enclosed within symbols. Speed also negates the possibility of being totally in command of the effect of one's actions, and it becomes an imperative to disregard their importance amidst everybody else's. The 'small cog in a big wheel' excuse, as it applies here, is an abdication of care.

'A great deal of today's art may be understood as motivated by a flight from interpretation. To avoid interpretation, art may become parody. Or it may become abstract. Or it may become ("merely") decorative. Or it may become non-art.

The flight from interpretation seems particularly a feature of modern painting. Abstract painting is the attempt to have, in the ordinary sense, no content; since there is no content, there can be no interpretation. Pop Art works by the opposite means to the same result; using a content so blatant, so "what it is", it, too, ends up being uninterpretable.'
(Susan Sontag, *Against Interpretation*, 1964, André Deutsch, 1987)

Sontag writes also of the interpreters' 'open aggressiveness' and their 'overt contempt for appearances'. How this applies in 1987 is through the need to make the distinction between critical challenge and monotonous diagnosis. The search for and the establishment of meanings that don't exist is the critic's driftwood; here, once again, we witness the elimination of risk, namely, the idea that there might be ideas that reach *beyond interpretation*. The media are thus able to maintain their position of control through their powers of explanation and simplification. The role of the writer or designer is to provide solutions, thereby fulfilling the public's expectation of their abilities — and to protect their own vested interests. To do otherwise is to invite ridicule. This is an extremely clever trade-off that has allowed the press and broadcasting cartel (in Britain at least) to concentrate its authority and the general public's pliability. The resultant cynicism constantly reinforces the status quo. This is one feature of what artists Margi Clarke and Jamie Reid have called 'Media Sickness — More Contagious Than Aids'.

As we now find ourselves in an age where the dominant forms of expression project themselves not from the voice to the ear, but to the eye, design is a great deal more pervasive than is suggested by its primary function of preparing artwork for the printer, or even blueprints for an architect. Design is also a means of connecting the increasingly disparate strands of the passing age of typography, with the emergent visual age of fibre-optic technology and microfilm storage. Technology insists that all history — as seen on TV — is now recent history. When it is used to form disparate strands of information into some kind of order, design is applied too often by those who have little understanding of the different elements involved. The short-cut is all important.

Design thus becomes a process of stasis and entropy, a blind attempt to defer the inevitable consequences of social and ecological irresponsibility. A parallel between the industrial revolution and the technological revolution is that both are geared to social control. As information increasingly becomes based on the language of airports and computer terminals, the role of design has never been more crucial, nor more widely abused.

A Chinese proverb says 'One hundred tellings are not as good as one seeing'. Design is a language, but looking at the conglomeration of styles in every main shopping centre in the world, it is plain that its currency is fleeting and its methods *seem* arbitrary. For commercial areas whose very existence depends on the novelty of their window displays, this is of course nothing new. Products have to be packaged and advertised in order to make them commercially viable, but what is most questionable is not the existence of advertising and packaging — 'the best of all possible worlds' has yet to be found — but the extremes to which both have degenerated. What is new is their level of exploitation, and the way in which the volume of their coverage has encouraged the new morality — the lust for personal wealth. Meanwhile, the present British government points to consumerism's victims as being 'the enemy within'; indeed, such suffering is viral.

When words and symbols are used as recognition factors in an attempt to consolidate this 'common language' (for example, with the 'Tell Sid' advertising campaign to promote shares in British Gas), what we are left with might indeed be common, but it is also deeply exclusive — the prerogative of business interests. Commerce needs to reduce all complicated ideas to a single colour to eliminate any possibility of missing its messages (just as muzak's moods are coded as 'red', 'green' or 'blue' to cover every aspect of human emotion). Signification is an easy way to codify (and neutralise) complex and potentially threatening ideas and cultural tendencies. It is small wonder that the obvious becomes obscure when so many words and visual symbols used in advertising have no meaning, yet convey countless insinuations.

People now more or less expect to be manipulated, even if many are unaware of how far-reaching this process has become. When so much communication is based on economic motives rather than personal interaction, this is hardly surprising. It is all to tempting to give in to 'the inevitable', whatever that is. What is missing is a sense of balance; the balance that is created from a position of critical objectivity *and* response, and the balance created from an equal consideration of the lessons of the past, the 'reality' of the present, and how these will, in turn, determine the future. Anything can happen.

BIBLIOGRAPHY

In addition to the works mentioned in the text, the following, listed in alphabetical order by title, are of interest:

After Babel George Steiner (Oxford University Press)

The Devil Tree Jerzy Kosinski (Arrow)

El Lissitsky S. Lissitsky-Kuppers (Thames and Hudson)

In Bluebeard's Castle George Steiner (Faber and Faber)

Jude The Obscure Thomas Hardy (Penguin)

Minutes To Go Burroughs/Corso/Gysin (Beach Books, San Francisco)

Painting Photography Film Laszlo Moholy-Nagy (Lund Humphries)

The Palette and The Flame — Posters of the Spanish Civil War, ed. John Tisa (Collet's)

Photo Eye Roh & Tschichold (Editions du Chêne, Paris)

Revolutionary Soviet Film Posters Constantine and Fern (The Johns Hopkins University Press)

Revues de Depero (Jean-Michel Place)

Rhyme & Reason: A Typographic Novel Erik Spiekermann (Berthold, Berlin)

The Sex Pistols Jon Savage (Faber and Faber)

Society of the Spectacle Guy Débord (Black and Red, Detroit)

Sounds Wassily Kandinsky (Yale University Press)

Subculture Dick Hebdige (Methuen)

Touch the Earth — A Portrait of Indian Life T. C. McLuhan (Abacus)

20th Century Posters: Design of the Avant-Garde (Abbeville)

We Yevgeny Zamyatin (Penguin)

Working Studs Terkel (Penguin)

ACKNOWLEDGMENTS

Full publication details appear in individual captions. Previously published copyright designs are reproduced by kind permission of the following:

9 Virgin Records Ltd
10 Stiff Records Ltd
11, 12, 467-471, 473 Touch
13 Seymour Productions/Naomi Grynn
15 Kopf
16 Demop
17, 50-81, 231-365 *The Face*/Wagadon Ltd
18-24 Demob
25, 26 Harvey Nichols & Co. Ltd
28 One Off
29 Fred Bare
30 Comag Ltd
32 Fwa Richards
33 Axco Instruments/M. M. Brody
34, 47, 48, 177-179, 195-197, 200 Phonogram Records (UK) Ltd
35, 36 Manor Jazz Festivals Ltd
37-44, 213, 221-225, 454, 455 Museum of Modern Art, Oxford
45, 158-164, 173, 174 Virgin Records Ltd/ Some Bizarre
46, 126-144, 201-207 Rod Pearce/ Fetish Records
49 Chrysalis Records
82, 83, 457 Claudia Josephs
85 The Big Club, Turin
86 Torchsong
87-91 Doublevision
92-94, 198 London Records Ltd
95 Artists Against Apartheid
96-98 Red Wedge
99 Campaign for Nuclear Disarmament
100-103, 366-376 *New Socialist*
104-106 Hyper Hyper
107,108 David Rosen/Pilcher Hershman
109 Panny Charrington
110-116 Norrie McLaren/Dont Flex
120-123 North Wing
124 The Monotype Corporation
125, 429-453 *Arena*/Wagadon Ltd
145, 148-150, 153-157, 165-169 Rough Trade Records Ltd
146, 147, 151, 152 Les Disques du Crépuscule
175, 176 EMI Records Ltd
180, 181 Hannibal Records Ltd
182, 183 Polydor Records Ltd
185 Mute Records Ltd
187 Crammed Discs
188-194 Oval Records
199 Don't Fall Off The Mountain/Beggars Banquet
208, 209, 211, 212 Illuminated Records Ltd
210 B.C. Records
214 Faber and Faber Ltd
215 Vermilion
216-219 Penguin Books Ltd
220 Omnibus Press
226 Comedia/Methuen Ltd
227 Elm Tree Books/Hamish Hamilton Ltd
228-230 Condé Nast Publications
377-428 *City Limits*/London Voice
447-453 IPC Magazines Ltd
456, 458, 459 Royal Court Theatre
460/461 Paul Webster
462-466 The Photographers' Gallery
474 Post